CRANIUM CRACKERS
BOOK 4

Anita Harnadek

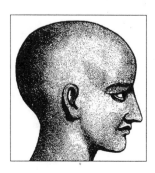

© 1991, 1997
CRITICAL THINKING BOOKS & SOFTWARE
www.criticalthinking.com
P.O. Box 448 • Pacific Grove • CA 93950-0448
Phone 800-458-4849 • FAX 831-393-3277
ISBN 0-89455-667-3
Printed in the United States of America

ACKNOWLEDGMENTS

Many thanks to my next-door neighbor, Eric Dueweke, who was just starting the third grade and who willingly agreed to read some of these materials in order to see if he understood them. His comments resulted in several simplifications and improvements. Thanks also to his parents, Mary and Joseph, for their ready cooperation in allowing me to enlist Eric's help.

Mrs. Anderson, the principal of Elmwood Elementary School in South Lake School District, St. Clair Shores, Michigan, has my gratitude for her rundown of the kinds of arithmetic taught in grades 3–4 and 5–6.

Table of Contents

Reference

Classroom Quickies, Books 2–3

CROSSING A RIVER

PROBLEM

1. A purple man with a purple dog, a green man with a green dog, and a striped man with a striped dog all want to get across a river filled with poisonous fish.

   They have a boat that will hold only two things at a time (two men, two dogs, or a man and a dog).

   None of the dogs can row.

   The men are very jealous about their dogs. No man is allowed near another man's dog unless either

   (1) the first man's dog is also there, or

   (2) the second man is also there.

   For example, suppose the green man and his dog are safely across the river with the boat, and the other two men and their dogs are still on the other side of the river. When the green man goes back, he cannot take either of the other dogs across, because neither condition (1) nor (2) would hold.

   How do they all get across if

   a. all three men can row?

   b. only one of the men can row?

Reference

Classroom Quickies, Books 1–3

REARRANGE LETTERS

DIRECTIONS

Use the letters at the top to fill in the chart so that words are formed and the sentence makes sense.

A shaded space in the chart shows the end of a word. Two shaded spaces together show the end of a sentence.

Except for the last line, the end of a line is not the end of a word unless there is a shaded space there.

When you have filled in the chart, answer the question asked.

PROBLEM

2.

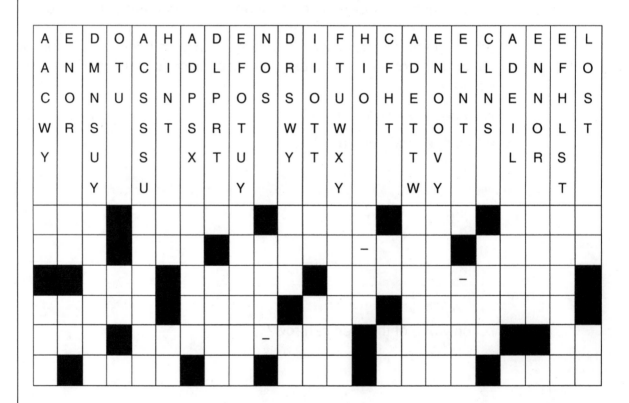

MISCELLANEOUS PROBLEMS

PROBLEMS

3. If a new car costs $20,000, what will be the cost of 4 tires at $75 each?

4. If a new car probably, but not necessarily, costs $20,000, what will be the cost of 4 tires at $75 each?

5. If a new car probably doesn't, but might, cost $20,000, what will be the cost of 4 tires at $75 each?

6. If a new car does not cost $20,000, what will be the cost of 4 tires at $75 each?

7. If a used car costs $20,000, what will be the cost of 4 tires at $75 each?

Reference

*Math
Word
Problems*

8. A billion dollars is a lot of money. Suppose you had a billion dollars.

a. How much interest would it earn in one year at 6%?

b. Suppose you left the billion dollars and the interest invested at 6% for another year. How much interest would be earned the second year?

c. How much interest is that for the two years?

d. Suppose you decided to count the original billion dollars, a dollar a second, day and night, never stopping to do anything else until you finished.

You couldn't keep it up indefinitely, so you can have five friends to help you out. (The interest will pay for their salaries.) You divide a 24-hour period into six 4-hour shifts. You and your friends each take one shift a day, so the counting still goes on day and night, one dollar per second.

About how old will you be when the billion dollars has all been counted? (Late teens? Early twenties? Or what?)

9. If you want to multiply a whole number by 25, you can tack on a couple of 0's and divide by 4.

   For example, $12 \times 25 = 1200/4 = 300$. And $17 \times 25 = 1700/4 = 425$.

   How come this works? (Or doesn't it? Did I just pick two examples that happened to work?)

10. If you want to multiply a whole number by 5, you can tack on a zero and divide by 2.

    For example, $26 \times 5 = 260/2 = 130$. And $38 \times 5 = 380/2 = 190$.

    How come this works? (Or doesn't it? Did I just pick two examples that happened to work?)

Reference

*Math
Word
Problems*

LIGHT-YEARS

DIRECTIONS

A **light-year** is the distance light travels in a year at a speed of 186,281.7 miles a second.[1]

If you compute with a calculator (or computer), use 186,281.7 miles a second for the speed of light, and use $365\frac{1}{4}$ days for a year.

If you have to do everything by hand, use 186,000 miles a second and 365 days.

PROBLEMS

11. How far is a light-year?

12. How long would it take a space ship traveling at a million miles an hour to go one light-year?

13. Alpha Centauri is the star (other than our sun) that is the nearest to Earth. Actually, Alpha Centauri is a cluster of three stars, named Alpha Centauri A, Alpha Centauri B, and Alpha Centauri C. Alpha Centauri C revolves around the other two. Because it comes closer to our sun than either of them, it is also called Proxima Centauri (the nearest star of Centaurus).

Proxima Centauri is about 4.3 light-years from us.

a. How many miles away from us is Proxima Centauri?

b. If Proxima Centauri exploded today, how long would it be before people on Earth could know about it?

---

1. This is the speed of light in a vacuum. Interstellar space is so empty that any difference between actual speed and speed in a vacuum is not considered to be significant.

Reference

*Math
Word
Problems*

INDEX OF REFRACTION

LESSON

Light does not travel through a medium (air or water, for instance) at the same speed as it travels in a vacuum.

To find the speed of light in a medium, we divide light's speed in a vacuum by a number called the <u>index of refraction</u> of the medium.

For example, if a medium has an index of refraction of $1\frac{1}{5}$, the speed of light through this medium would be (in miles per second) $186{,}000 \div 1\frac{1}{5} =$ $186{,}000 \div (6/5) = 186{,}000 \times \frac{5}{6} = 155{,}000$.

DIRECTIONS FOR PROBLEM 14

For this problem, use 186,000 miles a second as the speed of light in a vacuum. Give your answers to the nearest whole mile per second.

The problem tells you what the medium is and what the index of refraction is. Find the speed of light in that medium.

PROBLEM

14.   a.   water; index of refraction = $1\frac{3}{10}$

       b.   glass; index of refraction = $1\frac{1}{2}$

       c.   diamond; index of refraction = $2\frac{2}{5}$

PROBLEMS

15.   Can an index of refraction be less than 1? Explain.

Reference

*Math
Word
Problems*

16. Here are the mediums and their indexes of refraction again, this time given in decimal form.

water, 1.3

glass, 1.5

diamond, 2.4

Answer to the nearest .1%. At what percent of its speed in a vacuum does light travel through

a. water?

b. glass?

c. diamond?

Reference

Classroom Quickies, Books 1–3

WATER JUGS PROBLEMS

PROBLEM

17. You have 3 water jugs.

They hold, respectively, 4, 7, and 11 gallons.

They are unmarked, so you can't tell how much water is in them just by looking at them (unless they are full).

The 11-gallon jug is full. There is no other water supply.

Tell how you can get two measures, one of exactly 6 gallons and one of exactly 5 gallons.

Prove that a school cafeteria meal is better than complete happiness in life.

Reference

*Basic
Thinking
Skills*

FANTASY OR TRUE TO LIFE?

DIRECTIONS

A few statements are given to start a story. Accept these statements as true.

These statements are followed by some lettered statements. Decide whether the lettered statements sound true to life, or whether they sound more like fantasy.

EXAMPLE

Problem:

Diane had a very intelligent cat named Tiger.

Diane taught Tiger to walk for a short distance on his hind legs.

She also taught him to sit up and to shake hands.

a. Tiger could tell from the way Diane acted that she disliked his sharpening his claws on the furniture, so he stopped doing that and instead sharpened his claws on a tree when Diane let him go outside.

b. Tiger got bored with playing with a ball of string, so he found Diane's crochet hook and crocheted a small doily from the string.

Answers:

a. true to life

b. fantasy

PROBLEMS

18. Katina, 16 years old, was an outstanding athlete and was on her school's teams for swimming, volleyball, baseball, field hockey, track, and tennis. One day the school's Director of Athletics called her into his office and said, "I know

   a. how you love sports, but you can't continue to neglect your academic subjects. If you don't start studying more, your low grades are going to make you ineligible for our teams."

   b. you've worked hard at being a good athlete, but your attitude of superiority is causing friction on your teams. My concern is for the good of all students on the teams, and if your attitude doesn't change for the better, I'm going to recommend that you be dropped from at least some of the teams."

   c. the head coach for the U.S. Olympic track team, and on the basis of my recommendation he has agreed that you'll be on the next U.S. Olympic team."

   d. the editor of *Sports Illustrated*, and on the basis of what I've told him about you, he has agreed to send a reporter and a photographer here to interview you."

   e. you haven't decided yet about college, but the head coach at Stanford University called me today to ask about you. After what I told him, he said he'd like you to leave high school at the end of this semester and enroll at Stanford as an 'early admission' student because he wants you on the Stanford teams."

Reference

Basic Thinking Skills

19. Leona didn't understand today's mathematics lesson. The teacher had already said what they were going to study tomorrow, and Leona didn't see how she could understand that if she didn't understand today's lesson, so she

   a. stayed after school to get extra help from the teacher, and then she understood the lesson.

   b. asked her big brother for help with it, but she still didn't understand the lesson when he was through explaining it to her.

   c. told her dog, King, about it and showed him her mathematics book. King read the material and then explained it to Leona so that she understood it.

   d. said, "Oh, I wish some good angel would appear and explain it to me!" A good angel appeared and explained it to her, and Leona understood the lesson.

   e. said, "Oh, I wish I had a fairy godmother who'd make me smart enough to understand this!" But no fairy godmother appeared, and Leona still didn't understand the lesson when she went back to school the next day.

   f. gave up trying to understand it. She picked numbers out of thin air for the answers to the fifteen homework problems, and when the homework was checked in class the next day, every one of Leona's answers turned out to be right.

   g. concentrated very hard the next day on the new lesson, and she understood every bit of it, even though she still didn't understand the previous lesson, and even though the new lesson was based on the previous lesson.

Reference

Critical Thinking, Books 1 & 2

COUNTEREXAMPLES

Some statements are false but cannot be proved false. For example, suppose I told you that I've always wanted a zebra. I haven't, but there is no way for you to prove that I lied to you.

Other statements are false and <u>can</u> be proved false. For instance, suppose I said that everyone wants a zebra. My words will be proved false if you find one person who does <u>not</u> want a zebra.

That one person will be a **counterexample** to my statement.

A **counterexample** to a statement is a <u>specific</u> example that proves the statement is false.

EXAMPLE

Statement: Every dog is green.

These are counterexamples:

My dog is pink.

My sister's dog isn't green.

Ms. MacDonald's dog is orange with black spots.

These are not counterexamples:

I don't believe that. (No example is given.)

No dog is green. (No example is given.)

My cat is black. (This doesn't make the statement false.)

No bulldog is green. (This proves the statement false, but it is not a counterexample because it is not a <u>specific</u> example.)

Only certain kinds of statements can have counterexamples to them. (The next lesson will say more about this.) For these kinds of statements, counterexamples are nearly always the easiest way to prove the statements are not true.

Reference

*Critical
Thinking,
Books 1
& 2*

DIRECTIONS

A statement is given and is followed by several lettered sentences.

Tell whether or not each lettered sentence is a counterexample to the statement, and tell why.

PROBLEM

20.   Statement: No prime number is an even number.

   a.   4 isn't a prime number.

   b.   17 is a prime number.

   c.   15 isn't a prime number.

   d.   No prime number is a multiple of 9.

   e.   2 is a prime number.

   f.   There is no largest prime number, so how do you know that one of the large ones isn't even?

   g.   Not all odd numbers are prime numbers.

   h.   6 is a prime number.

Reference

*Critical
Thinking,
Books 1
& 2*

LESSON

A counterexample contradicts a statement about everything of a kind. This means that only certain kinds of statements can have counterexamples.

These statements are about everything of a kind. There may be counterexamples to these statements.

All dogs are green.

No dog is green.

If something is a dog, then it is green.

No single example will prove any of these next statements false, because the statements are not about everything of a kind. Such statements cannot have counterexamples.

Some dogs are green.

Many dogs are green.

Only a few dogs are green.

Notice that a counterexample to a statement proves that the statement is false in one case, but it doesn't prove the statement is false in every case.

In other words, a counterexample simply shows that the statement should not have been made about <u>everything</u>.

EXAMPLE

Statement: All dogs are green.

Counterexample: My dog isn't green.

The counterexample proves the statement false, but it doesn't prove that no dog is green.

Reference

Critical Thinking, Books 1 & 2

DIRECTIONS

Tell whether or not each lettered statement is the kind of statement for which a counterexample might be found.

In other words, tell whether or not the statement could be proved false by finding just one example.

PROBLEM

21. a. All states (in the U.S.) have compulsory school attendance laws.

b. Everybody in New York likes to watch football games on TV.

c. Most teenagers like pizza.

d. Not everyone knows how to drive a car.

e. Some rectangles are not squares.

f. Not all that glitters is gold.

g. If two odd numbers are added, then their sum is even.

h. If a four-digit number is divided by a two-digit number, the quotient is sometimes a two-digit number.

i. If a four-digit number is divided by a two-digit number, the quotient is sometimes a two-digit number, and the rest of the time the quotient is a one-digit number.

Reference

Critical Thinking, Books 1 & 2

DIRECTIONS

A statement is given and is followed by lettered sentences. Tell whether or not each lettered sentence is a counterexample to the statement. If it is not, then tell why not.

EXAMPLE

Problem: All boys like to play baseball.

    a. Brad is a boy, and he doesn't like to play baseball.

    b. Cathy is a girl, and she likes to play baseball.

Answers: a. Yes

        b. No. The statement does not say anything about what girls like or don't like.

PROBLEMS

22. Hand calculators should be allowed in all math classes.

    a. Not everyone can afford a hand calculator.

    b. A hand calculator isn't of any use in a computer programming class.

    c. Mr. Browne won't permit the students to use hand calculators in his algebra class.

23. Every notably intelligent person has a highly developed sense of humor.

    a. That's because they're smart enough to see how ridiculous so many things are.

    b. My neighbor has a highly developed sense of humor, and he isn't very intelligent at all.

    c. My boss is extremely intelligent, but she hardly ever sees the funny side of something.

Reference

*Critical
Thinking,
Books 1
& 2*

24. Nearly all great mathematicians made significant mathematical discoveries when they were in their teens.

    a. Albert Einstein didn't make any significant mathematical discoveries until he was over twenty.

    b. Yes, but what were significant discoveries a hundred years and more ago are now often taught in high school classes. Students today don't have the same opportunities for discoveries because the field is no longer so undeveloped.

    c. Almost nothing is known about Euclid's life, so you can't claim that your statement applies to him.

25. Almost nobody wants to live in Antarctica for five years.

    a. I know a professor who wants to study the effects of extreme cold on various plants and animals, including humans. He'd love to live there for five years.

    b. Winter sports enthusiasts might not mind it.

26. If a teenager wants work, (s)he should be given a job.

    a. If you mean for no pay, then I agree. But if you mean for pay, who's going to pay out money and go through all the hassle of filing government forms for it just because someone else wants to earn some money?

    b. My fourteen-year-old sister wants to work, but she shouldn't be given a job, because she's clumsy and breaks things and has no sense of responsibility.

Reference

Critical Thinking, Books 1 & 2

27. Suppose a statement about everything of a kind is true.

Can there be a counterexample to it? If so, give an example. If not, how come?

28. Suppose you are given the statement

All zoffers are middigs,

and you find a zoffer that is not a middig.

a. Have you found a counterexample to the statement?

b. Have you proved the statement false?

c. Have you proved that no zoffers are middigs?

d. Have you proved that some (at least one) zoffers are not middigs?

e. Have you proved that if anything is a zoffer, then it is not a middig?

f. Have you proved that if anything is a zoffer, then it is not necessarily a middig?

g. Have you proved that if anything is not a zoffer, then it is a middig?

h. Have you proved that if anything is a middig, then it is not a zoffer?

i. Have you proved that some (at least one) middigs are not zoffers?

Reference

Critical Thinking, Books 1 & 2

29.   Suppose you are given the statement,

All zoffers are middigs,

and you find a middig that is not a zoffer.

a. Have you found a counterexample to the statement?

b. Have you proved the statement false?

c. Have you proved that no zoffers are middigs?

d. Have you proved that some (at least one) zoffers are not middigs?

e. Have you proved that if anything is a zoffer, then it is not a middig?

f.   Have you proved that if anything is a zoffer, then it is not necessarily a middig?

g. Have you proved that if anything is not a zoffer, then it is a middig?

h. Have you proved that if anything is not a zoffer, then it is not a middig?

i.   Have you proved that if anything is a middig, then it is not a zoffer?

j.   Have you proved that some (at least one) middigs are not zoffers?

Reference

Critical Thinking, Book 1

Inductive Thinking Skills

DRAWING INFERENCES

DIRECTIONS

You are given a short story. Tell whether each lettered sentence below the story is true (T), is false (F), or whether you need more information in order to decide (?).

Accept the story as true. Try to forget anything you heard before about the story. Assume the story uses good English. Try to place yourself in the setting of the story.

Use what you know unless the story says something different. For example, you know what a "house" is, but suppose the story says that only a blue tent can be a "house." Then you must believe the story, and you must not use your own idea of what a "house" is.

PROBLEMS

30. **Story**

LITTLE RED RIDING HOOD

Little Red Riding Hood's grandmother was ill, and Red decided to take her a basket of goodies to help her get well.

The big bad wolf saw Red walking through the woods on her way to the grandmother's house, and he ran all the way to the grandmother's house and disposed of the grandmother.

Although Red didn't recognize the wolf when she arrived at her grandmother's house, she screamed in time to be rescued by a nearby woodsman.

a. Red's grandmother is alive when the story starts.

b. Red's mother fixed the basket of goodies for Red to take.

c. Red recognized the wolf in time to be rescued.

[Problem continued on next page.]

Reference

Critical Thinking, Book 1

Inductive Thinking Skills

[Problem continued from previous page.]

d. Red was in the woods when the wolf saw her.

e. The wolf was in the woods when he saw Red.

f. Red was taking the goodies to her grandmother's house when the wolf saw her.

g. The wolf was bad.

h. Maybe Red saw the wolf in the woods at the same time that he saw her.

i. Red didn't like her grandmother.

j. Red ran all the way from her house to her grandmother's house.

[Problem continued on next page.]

Reference

Critical
Thinking,
Book 1

Inductive
Thinking
Skills

[Problem continued from previous page.]

k. Maybe Red had her bicycle with her.

l. Red noticed immediately that the wolf was not her grandmother.

m. Red couldn't have been in a hurry to get to her grandmother's house, or she would have been running, not walking, through the woods.

n. Red was rescued by a woodsman.

o. A woodsman heard Red's scream.

p. The wolf killed Red's grandmother.

Reference

*Critical
Thinking,
Book 1*

*Inductive
Thinking
Skills*

31.   Story

THE SLEEPING BEAUTY

Once upon a time there was a couple who was so poor that they wore rags and often had no food.

A witch came to them and said she would make them wealthy if they would give her their baby girl. They refused and the witch left, but she was very angry and said she'd make them sorry for refusing her offer.

The next day the man found a job, and he was so grateful and worked so hard that he soon got promoted. He and his wife and daughter prospered, but the man and his wife worried about what the wicked witch had said.

The wife taught their daughter to cook and spin and weave and sew, and the daughter grew into a beautiful young lady.

On the daughter's sixteenth birthday, one of her gifts was a gold spinning wheel, and she was so entranced by it that she had to try it out right away.

She had no sooner started spinning than a sharp spindle pricked her finger. She immediately fell into a deep sleep, for the spinning wheel had been sent by the witch, and the spindle had been dipped into a potent sleeping potion.

a.   The daughter is not beautiful when the story starts out.

b.   The witch who sent the spinning wheel is not the same witch as in the second paragraph.

[Problem continued on next page.]

Reference

Critical Thinking, Book 1

Inductive Thinking Skills

[Problem continued from previous page.]

c. The witch wanted the daughter to prick her finger on the spindle.

d. The witch wanted the daughter to fall into a deep sleep.

e. The witch was wicked.

f. The daughter fell into a deep sleep on her sixteenth birthday.

g. The daughter was conceited about her beauty.

h. The daughter liked spinning.

[Problem continued on next page.]

Reference

Critical Thinking, Book 1

Inductive Thinking Skills

[Problem continued from previous page.]

i.   The man and his wife loved their daughter.

j.   The daughter had a party on her sixteenth birthday.

k.   The girl's parents worried about what the witch had said.

l.   The girl slept for many years but was awakened by the kiss of a handsome prince.

Now make up some statements of your own for your classmates to judge as "T," "F," or "?." Try to make up at least one statement that you think your classmates will answer incorrectly.

Reference

*Critical
Thinking,
Book 1*

*Inductive
Thinking
Skills*

32.   Story

MIKLAS, ALTHAEA, STAVROS, AND HIPPO

Miklas is twice as old as his sister Althaea, who is three years older than her brother Stavros, who is four years older than his horse, Hippo, who is at least one year old.

a.   Miklas and Stavros are brothers.

b.   Miklas and Hippo are brothers.

c.   If Althaea is ten years old, then Hippo's age is two years.

d.   Stavros is five years old.

e.   Althaea is at least eight years old.

f.   Miklas is at least eleven years older than Stavros.

[Problem continued on next page.]

Reference

Critical Thinking, Book 1

Inductive Thinking Skills

[Problem continued from previous page.]

g. Hippo is Stavros's pet.

h. Hippo is at least seven years younger than Althaea.

i. Maybe Hippo is eight years younger than Althaea.

j. Althaea has a sister named Chrysoula.

k. Stavros is at least twenty years old.

l. Maybe Hippo is eighteen years old.

m. If Miklas is thirty years old, then Hippo's age is seven.

OPERATORS AND ORDER OF PRECEDENCE

LESSON

Addition (+), subtraction (–), multiplication (×), division (÷ or /), raising to a power (such as 3^2), and taking a square root (such as $\sqrt{25}$) are arithmetic **operators**.

A problem can include an operator more than once:

$$5 + 3 + 4 = ?$$

It can also include different operators:

$$5 + 3 - 4 = ?$$

$$1 + 2 \times 3 = ?$$

Parentheses can be used to show which operator to start with:

$$(1 + 2) \times 3 = ?$$

$$1 + (2 \times 3) = ?$$

Brackets can be used as a second set of parentheses:

$$15 - [12 - 3 \times (1 + 2)] = ?$$

Braces can be used as a third set of parentheses:

$$30 - \{3 - [17 - 5 \times (1 + 2)]\}$$

To solve a problem, we move from left to right, but we must do it in this order:

1. ( )

2. [ ]

3. { }

4. raise to a power, take a root [These operators are equal in rank. Start at the left and do whichever one comes first. Keep going and do whichever one comes next.]

5. ×, ÷ or / [These operators have equal rank.]

6. +, – [These operators have equal rank.]

For the examples below, remember the rules: move from left to right, but first do ( ), then [ ], then { }, then raise to a power or take a root, then × or ÷ or /, and then + or − .

EXAMPLE 1

Problem: $24 - (5 + 2) \times 3$

Solution: (Steps that are not needed are skipped here.)

Step 1.   Do ( ). So do $5 + 2$. So $24 - (5 + 2) \times 3 = 24 - 7 \times 3$.

Step 5.   Do ×, ÷, and /. There is no ÷ or /, so do 7×3 and get $24 - 7 \times 3 = 24 - 21$.

Step 6.   Do + and − . There is no +, so $24 - 21 = 3$.

Answer: $24 - (5 + 2) ¥ 3 = 24 - 7 ¥ 3 = 24 - 21 = 3$

EXAMPLE 2

Problem: $24 - (8 + 2 \times 5) \div 6$

Solution:

Step 1.   Do ( ). So do $8 + 2 \times 5$. Because × is done before +, we get $8 + 2 \times 5 = 8 + 10 = 18$. The problem is now $24 - 18 \div 6$.

Step 5.   Do ÷. So $24 - 18 \div 6 = 24 - 3$.

Step 6.   Do − . We get $24 - 3 = 21$.

Answer: $24 - (8 + 2 \times 5) \div 6 = 24 - (8 + 10) \div 6 = 24 - 18 \div 6 = 24 - 3 = 21$

EXAMPLE 3

Problem: $5 + 12/(1 + 3) \times 3$

Solution:

Step 1.   Do ( ). We get $5 + 12/(1 + 3) \times 3 = 5 + 12/4 \times 3$.

Step 5.   Do × and /. We go from left to right and get $5 + 12/4 \times 3 = 5 + 3 \times 3 = 5 + 9$.

Step 6.   Do +. We get $5 + 9 = 14$.

Answer: $5 + 12/(1 + 3) \times 3 = 5 + 12/4 \times 3 = 5 + 3 \times 3 = 5 + 9 = 14$

EXAMPLE 4

Problem: $14 - [6 \div 3 + 1 \times (2 + 3)]$

Solution: Notice that "÷" in the given problem is written as "/" below. The two symbols mean the same thing and can be freely exchanged.

Step 1. Do ( ). So do $2 + 3 = 5$. This makes the problem
$14 - [6/3 + 1 \times (2 + 3)] = 14 - [6/3 + 1 \times 5]$.

Step 2. Do [ ]. We work from left to right, doing / and × before +, so
$6/3 + 1 \times 5 = 2 + 1 \times 5 = 2 + 5 = 7$. Starting from the end of
Step 1 above, we now have $14 - [6/3 + 1 \times 5] = 14 - 7$.

Step 6. Do − . We get $14 - 7 = 7$.

Answer: $14 - [6 \div 3 + 1 \times (2 + 3)] =$
$14 - [6 \div 3 + 1 \times 5] =$
$14 - [2 + 1 \times 5] = 14 - [2 + 5] = 14 - 7 = 7$

EXAMPLE 5

Problem: $(3 + 12 \div 3) \times (6 - 4 + 2) - 4^2$

Solution:

Step 1. Do ( ). There are two sets of ( ). We work from left to right, so
first we will do $3 + 12 \div 3$, and then we will do $6 - 4 + 2$. We do
÷ before +, so for $3 + 12 \div 3$, we get $3 + 4 = 7$. Taking $6 - 4 +$
2, the + and − have equal rank, so we move left to right and
get $6 - 4 + 2 = 2 + 2 = 4$. We now have $(3 + 12 \div 3) \times (6 - 4 +$
$2) - 4^2 = 7 \times 4 - 4^2$.

Step 4. Do "raise to a power." So do $4^2 = 16$. The problem is now
$7 \times 4 - 4^2 = 7 \times 4 - 16$.

Step 5. Do ×. We get $7 \times 4 - 16 = 28 - 16$.

Step 6. Do −. So $28 - 16 = 12$.

Answer: $(3 + 12 \div 3) \times (6 - 4 + 2) - 4^2 =$
$(3 + 4) \times (6 - 4 + 2) - 4^2 =$
$7 \times (6 - 4 + 2) - 4^2 =$
$7 \times (2 + 2) - 4^2 =$
$7 \times 4 - 4^2 = 7 \times 4 - 16 = 28 - 16 = 12$

EXAMPLE 6

Problem: $20 \div 10/2 \times 7 \times 2^3$

Solution: We don't need Steps 1, 2, 3, or 6 for this one. Step 5 says the operators $\times$, $\div$, and / are all of equal rank and we are to work from left to right. We do Step 4 and then Step 5.

Answer: $20 \div 10/2 \times 7 \times 2^3 =$

$20 \div 10/2 \times 7 \times 8 =$

$2/2 \times 7 \times 8 = 1 \times 7 \times 8 = 7 \times 8 = 56$

Notice how the answer would change if ( ) enclosed 10/2. Then it would be

$20 \div (10/2) \times 7 \times 2^3 =$

$20 \div 5 \times 7 \times 2^3 =$

$20 \div 5 \times 7 \times 8 = 4 \times 7 \times 8 = 28 \times 8 = 224.$

DIRECTIONS

You are told what answer is wanted. To get this answer, you may use only the numbers 4, 8, and 12, along with two operators. You may NOT use ( ), [ ], or { }.

You are allowed to raise to a power or take a square root. Show your work in the same way the Example below shows the work.

EXAMPLE

Problem: Get an answer of 16.

Answer: $12 \times \sqrt{4} - 8 = 12 \times 2 - 8 = 24 - 8 = 16$

For each answer, you must use each of the numbers 4, 8, and 12 exactly once. You may use the same operator twice if you wish to do so.

There may be different ways to get an answer, but you need to find only one way.

You are not allowed to combine digits to make a new number. For example, you are not allowed to combine 4 and 8 and get 48. However, you are allowed to raise to a power or to take a root or to do both, such as $\sqrt{4}^{\,8}$.

PROBLEMS

33.   Get an answer of 0.

34.   Get an answer of 2.

35.   Get an answer of 4.

36.   Get an answer of 5.

37.   Get an answer of 6.

38.   Get an answer of 10.

39.   Get an answer of 12.

40.   Get an answer of 14.

41.   Get an answer of 18.

DIRECTIONS

Find the answer for each problem. Show your work.

PROBLEMS

42. $24/(6 - 2) + (7 - 3) \times 5$

43. $8 \times 3^2 - [21/(5 - 2) + 5 \times 11]$

44. $26 - [(9 - 5)^2 + 6]$

45. $6 \times 7 - (\sqrt{25} + 48/4/3)$

46. $\sqrt{4}^{\,3} \times (1 + 2 \times 3)$

47. $88 - \{4 + 5 \times [3 + 45/(7 + 2)]\}$

48. $48/2^3/2 + 4 \times 5 - (20 - 2 \times 8)$

49. $58 - \{5 + 2 \times 4 - [3 \times 12 - (4 \times 5 + 14)] + 2\}$

50.　$3^3 - (2^4 + \sqrt{25} + \sqrt{49} - 1)$

51.　$(2 \times 3 + 4)^2 + \sqrt{49} \times 2^3 - 1 - 5 \times (9 \times 5 - 1)/4 - 3^2 \times (7 + 4)$

52.　$\{9^2 - (3 \times 5 - 4) - [8^2 - (5 + 7) \times 2]\} \times \{19 - [(\sqrt{3 + 13})^2 + 1]\}$

DIRECTIONS

Insert ( ), [ ], and { } so that the problem's answer will be the answer given. If no { } are needed, then don't insert any. Likewise, if no [ ] are needed, or if no ( ) are needed, then don't insert any.

Show your work as the examples do.

EXAMPLE 1

Problem: $1 + 4 \times 3 + 2$; answer 21

Answer: $1 + 4 \times (3 + 2) = 1 + 4 \times 5 = 1 + 20 = 21$

EXAMPLE 2

Problem: $1 + 4 \times 3 + 2$; answer 15

Answer: $1 + 4 \times 3 + 2 = 1 + 12 + 2 = 13 + 2 = 15$

PROBLEMS

53. $5 + 3 \times 2 - 4 + 1$; answer 11

54. $4^2 - 2 + 3 \times 3$; answer 1

55. $4 \times 11 + 3 + 2 \times 5 - 6$; answer 51

56. $17 - 25 - 1 + 3 \times 5$; answer 12

57. $48/3^2 - 1 + 7 - 5 \times 6$; answer 18

58. $36/3 \times 12/4/2$; answer 2

59. $5 \times 3 + 2 \times 3 - 5^2 \times 5$; answer 100

60. $39/5^2 - 4^2/3 - 2 \times 5$; answer 3

61.　$3 \times 5 \times 7 + 5 + 4 \times 6 + 7 - 6 \times 11$; answer 30

62.　$10 - 7 \times 4 - 2 \times 3^2 - 2^3 - 4$; answer 6

63.　$7 \times 158 - 2 - 7 \times 6 + 2 - 3 \times 5^2 - 2 \times 9 + 1$; answer 56

64. You are given three numbers.

a. Suppose you subtract the second from the first, and then you subtract the third from that answer.

Tell why the final result is the same as adding the last two and subtracting that sum from the first.

b. Suppose you subtract the third from the second and then subtract the result from the first.

Tell why the final answer is the same as subtracting the second from the first and then adding the third to that result.

c. Suppose you subtract the second number from the first and then add the third number to that result.

Tell why the final answer is the same as adding the first and third numbers and then subtracting the second number from that result.

d. Suppose you subtract the second number from the first and then subtract the third number from that result.

Tell why the final answer is the same as subtracting the third number from the first and then subtracting the second number from that result.

The problems could be stated this way:

For any three numbers r, s, and t,

a. $(r - s) - t = r - (s + t)$. Or, $r - s - t = r - (s + t)$.

b. $r - (s - t) = (r - s) + t$. Or, $r - (s - t) = r - s + t$.

c. $(r - s) + t = (r + t) - s$. Or, $r - s + t = r + t - s$.

d. $(r - s) - t = (r - t) - s$. Or, $r - s - t = r - t - s$.

Reference

Classroom Quickies, Books 1–3

65. Using the digits 1, 2, 3, and 4 along with any mathematical operators you choose, see how many different numbers you can write.

Here are the rules:

Your answers must be whole numbers.

In each answer, you must use each of the four digits exactly once.

You are allowed to use any mathematical symbols and operators you know about. For example, you may use decimals, and if you know about logarithms or summation symbols, you may use those, too.

In each answer, you may use any operator as often as you like.

You are allowed to use each digit as a separate number.

You are allowed to combine two or more digits to make a number.

If you combine two digits to make a number, you cannot use an operator to separate the digits. For example, you may use 1 and 2 to make the number 21, but you may not write something like

$$2(4 - 3)$$

to make 21, or like

$$1\sqrt{4}$$

to make 12. However, you ARE allowed to use a decimal point between two digits. For example, you could write

$$1.2$$

to make one and two tenths.

EXAMPLES

$$0 = 1 + 4 - 2 - 3$$

$$1 = 2 \times 3 - 4 - 1$$

$$2 = (2 + 4) \div 3 \times 1$$

$$3 = (4 + 2) \times 1 - 3$$

$$4 = 2^3 \div \sqrt{4} \times 1$$

$$5 = (4^2 - 1)/3$$

$$6 = 12/4 + 3$$

Reference

Classroom Quickies. Books 1–3

66. This problem is like the preceding one, except that this time you are to use only 4's, along with any mathematical operators you choose.

For each problem, you must use at least two 4's, and you may not use more than six 4's.

See how many different numbers you can write.

Here are the rules again:

Your answers must be whole numbers.

You are allowed to use any mathematical symbols and operators you know about. For example, you may use decimals, and if you know about logarithms or summation symbols, you may use those, too.

In each answer, you may use any operator as often as you like.

You are allowed to use each 4 as a separate number.

You are allowed to combine two or more 4's to make a number.

If you combine two or more 4's to make a number, you cannot use an operator to separate the digits. For example, you may use two 4's to make the number 44, but you may not write something like

$$4(4 + 4 - 4) \qquad \text{or} \qquad 4\sqrt{4 \times 4}$$

to make 44. However, you ARE allowed to use a decimal point between two digits. For example, you could write

$$4.4$$

to make four and four tenths.

EXAMPLES

$$0 = 4 - 4$$

$$1 = 4 \div 4$$

$$2 = (4 + 4)/4$$

$$3 = 4 - 4/4$$

$$4 = 4 \times 4/4$$

$$5 = 4 + 4/4$$

$$6 = \sqrt{4} \times \sqrt{4} + (4 + 4)/4$$

INEQUALITIES AND THEIR NEGATION

LESSON

You have seen these symbols before:

> (greater than)

< (less than).

We can combine either of them with = like this, $\gtreqless$, but they are usually written

≥ (greater than or equal to)

≤ (less than or equal to).

A slash (/ or \) through a relation symbol negates (denies) the relation. Here are some examples:

= (equal to), ≠ (not equal to)
[In computer programming, there is no ≠ symbol.
Instead, <> (either less than or greater than) is used.]

|| (parallel to), ∦ (not parallel to)

⊥ (perpendicular to), ⊥̸ (not perpendicular to)

⇒ (implies), ⇏ (does not imply)

> (greater than), ≯ (not greater than)

≥ (greater than or equal to),
≱ (neither greater than nor equal to; not greater than and not equal to)

< (less than), ≮ (not less than)

≤ (less than or equal to),
≰ (neither less than nor equal to; not less than and not equal to)

DIRECTIONS

Tell whether each statement is true or false. Show your work.

EXAMPLE

Problem: $18 - 5 < 10 \times 2$

Answer: $13 < 20$; true

PROBLEMS

67.　$3 \times 6 > 9 + 8$

68.　$11 \times 3 \le 3 \times 9$

69.　$44 - 20 \le 2 \times 12$

70.　$4 \times 9 \not< 2 \times 10$

71. $3 + 6 \ngeq 3 \times 6$

72. $22 + 33 - 5 \times 5 \ngeq 3 \times 10$

73. $15 + 5 - 4 \neq 14 + 7 - 5$

74. $4 \times (10 - 3) <> 3 \times 8$

75. $2^3 \leq 3^2$

76. $3^4 \leq 4^3$

DIRECTIONS

You are given two expressions and three symbols.

Simplify each expression and choose the correct symbol to place between the results.

Leave the expressions in the order they are given. (Don't exchange the order.)

Show your work.

EXAMPLE 1

Problem: 3×4; $5 \times 8 - 50/5$; $<, \leq, >$

Answer: $3 \times 4 = 12$; $5 \times 8 - 50/5 = 40 - 10 = 30$; $12 < 30$

[Don't switch 30 and 12 and get $30 > 12$.]

If more than one of the given symbols can be used, then show your answer for all such symbols.

EXAMPLE 2

Problem: 3×4; $20 - 7$; $\leq, \neq, \ngeq$

Answer: $3 \times 4 = 12$; $20 - 7 = 13$; $12 \leq 13$; $12 \neq 13$; $12 \ngeq 13$

PROBLEMS

77. $20 + 55$; $3 \times 12 + 10$; $<, \leq, >$

78. $28 - 3 \times 7$; $49 - 5 \times 9$; $<, \nleq, =$

79. $36/3 + 8$; $35 - 3 \times 5$; $<, \nleq, =$

80. $4 \times 5 + 6$; $3 \times 12 - 14$; $\nleq$, $\geq$, $=$

81. $70 - 4 \times 5$; 2×5^2; $\leq$, $\ngeq$, $>$

82. 4×5; $60 - 40/8 - 5 \times 11$; $\nless$, $\neq$, $\ngtr$

83. $4 + 5 \times [24/(2 + 6) + 1]$; $3 \times 5 - (24/4 + 6)$; $\geq$, $\ngeq$, $\nleq$

84. $[24/(5 + 1) + 2]/3$; $4 \times 8 - (3 \times 5 + 10)$; $\neq$, $\ngeq$, $\nleq$

Reference

*Inductive
Thinking
Skills*

RELEVANT INFORMATION

LESSON

Suppose you are thinking about whether or not to get your hair cut.

You tell your friend James, and he makes a comment.

If his comment is supposed to help you reach a decision, then his comment is **relevant** (REL uh vuhnt). Otherwise, his comment is irrelevant or not relevant.

EXAMPLE

Problem: Should you get your hair cut, or not?

Relevant comments from James:

You look better with your hair as it is now.

Will you have enough money to pay for it?

Your hair is too long now.

Your hair isn't long enough now.

Irrelevant comments, or comments that are not relevant:

My brother got his hair cut yesterday.

You have brown eyes.

My mother always cuts my hair.

You got your hair cut two weeks ago, didn't you?

We say that a statement (or question) is **relevant** to a subject if that statement (or question) has a bearing upon the subject.

A relevant statement (or question) always has a logical connection with the subject.

Reference

*Inductive
Thinking
Skills*

DIRECTIONS

A problem is stated and is followed by several lettered sentences.

For each lettered sentence, tell whether or not it is relevant to the problem.

PROBLEMS

85. Richard, who lives in southern Michigan, is going to plant vegetables around the edges of his parents' back yard.

    It is now February. Frost in Richard's area sometimes occurs as late as the middle of May and as early as late October, leaving a growing season of about 160 days.

    Richard, looking through a seed catalog with his friend Javier, is trying to decide what kinds of vegetable seeds to order.

    Here are some of Javier's comments.

    a. What vegetables do you and your family like best?

    b. The catalog will tell you whether or not the seeds and plants can stand frost.

    c. How many different kinds of seeds will you plant?

    d. You can plant seeds indoors next month and then put the plants outdoors in May.

[Problem continued on next page.]

Reference

Inductive
Thinking
Skills

[Problem continued from previous page.]

e. You could plant a thin line of flower seeds in front of the vegetables so that the yard would look nicer.

f. What kind of soil will you use?

g. Make a list of all the seeds you think you'd like to get, and then eliminate the ones that take too long or too much room to grow.

h. I think I'll plant a garden in our back yard, too.

i. You're going to have a lot of work. You'll have to dig a bed for the seeds and then keep it weeded and watered all summer.

j. Your back yard is sunny practically all day, so you can forget about vegetables that grow well only in partial shade.

Reference

*Inductive
Thinking
Skills*

86. Melissa, 15 years old and starting the tenth grade, wants to learn to repair computers and printers when she leaves high school. She plans to attend a technical training school and then get a job as a repair person.

She intends to save whatever she earns between now and the time she graduates from high school so that she will be able to pay for the training school and meet living expenses while she is training.

Melissa asked some of her friends to suggest ways she might earn enough money to reach her goal. Here are some of the comments her friends made.

a. Fast-food restaurants are often looking for help.

b. State law says that most businesses can't hire you without a work permit while you're in school, and you can't get one of those until you're 16.

c. You make most of your own clothes. Maybe you could make or alter clothes for other people.

d. If you get a regular job, the law allows you to work only a certain number of hours each week.

e. Take typing and shorthand classes next year and then get a summer job working in an office.

f. That's too much money for you to earn in just three years of part-time work.

[Problem continued on next page.]

[Problem continued from previous page.]

Reference

*Inductive
Thinking
Skills*

g. There's a library book that lists all kinds of jobs.

h. Make up a ditto master and run off copies. Put your name and telephone number on it. Say you're looking for odd jobs, and list a few—like window washing, cleaning basements and garages, washing walls, mowing lawns, baby-sitting, whatever. Go to every house in your neighborhood and introduce yourself and leave a copy with whoever you talk to.

i. People never want to hire teenagers.

j. You should find out if the training school gives scholarships and if you could qualify for one. Then you wouldn't need so much money.

k. Instead of that out-of-town school, why don't you settle for a career you can get local training for? Then you could live at home and not need so much money.

l. Computer technology changes so fast that the training you'll get at your school will be outdated within a year. You'll have wasted your money.

m. You should write to some computer companies and see if they have any "earn while you learn" plans. Maybe you could get your training free from one of them.

Reference

*Inductive
Thinking
Skills*

87. Hiro's class was trying to think of things that still need to be invented.

Here are some of the comments made by Hiro and his classmates.

a. All really worthwhile things have already been invented. There's nothing left to invent that would be of any great use.

b. We need a faucet washer that would last years and years. The washers at my house have to be replaced at least once a year.

c. How about a self-repairing car engine?

d. People today are just as creative as people were years ago, but there isn't as much to be creative about.

e. Think how much tax money would be saved if there were a paint that would bond with pavement so that road lanes would need to be marked off only when the pavement is laid.

[Problem continued on next page.]

Reference

Inductive
Thinking
Skills

[Problem continued from previous page.]

f. How about pavement that doesn't break up from traffic?

g. Someone should invent a gas furnace that is at least 90% efficient at burning the gas it uses.

h. We should have pedestrian roads made so that the lanes move. Have maybe six lanes ranging from five to thirty miles an hour. Then we could go places without cars or buses.

i. Some new inventions might be convenient, but that doesn't automatically mean these inventions are needed.

j. Wouldn't it be great if there was a kind of makeup machine so that a woman could dial a number on it and it would make up her face just like the makeup used for a picture whose number corresponds with the number dialed?

Reference

Math
Word
Problems

AREAS

PROBLEMS

88. You are given a 9 in. × 12 in. rectangle that has a border 2 in. wide.

   A. If the border is inside the given rectangle, what is the area of

      a. the rectangle enclosed within the border?

      b. the border?

   B. If the border is outside the given rectangle, what is the area of

      a. the outer rectangle (the rectangle that encloses the border)?

      b. the border?

Reference

*Math
Word
Problems*

Free information:

The circumference of a circle is $C = \pi d$

The area of a circle is $A = \pi r^2$

π is about $3\frac{1}{7}$ or, more exactly, about 3.1416.

89. For this problem, don't use π's approximate value. That is, just write π instead of $3\frac{1}{7}$ or 3.1416.

Circle #1 has a diameter of 20 in.

Inside circle #1 is circle #2, with a diameter of 18 in.

Inside circle #2 is circle #3, with a diameter of 16 in.

Inside circle #3 is circle #4, with a diameter of 14 in.

A. If the circles all have the same center, what is the area of the ring whose borders are circles #

   a. 1 and 2?

   b. 3 and 4?

   c. 1 and 3?

   d. 1 and 4?

   e. 2 and 4?

[Problem continued on next page.]

Reference

Math
Word
Problem

[Problem continued from previous page.]

   B. Suppose that no two of the circles have the same center.

       What is the area enclosed between circles #

       a. 1 and 2?

       b. 3 and 4?

       c. 1 and 3?

       d. 1 and 4?

       e. 2 and 4?

Handbooks used by engineers usually give π to at least ten places, 3.1415926536. For practical purposes, this is so accurate that if the earth's diameter were 8,000 miles, the difference between using π to ten places and π to eleven places to figure the earth's circumference would make a difference of less than $\frac{1}{100}$ inch. (π to eleven places is 3.14159265359.)

MISCELLANEOUS PROBLEM

PROBLEM

90.   If you want to divide a whole number by 5, you can multiply it by 2 and insert a decimal point just before the last digit.

EXAMPLES

To divide 23 by 5, take $23 \times 2 = 46$ and put a decimal point before the 6, getting 4.6.

To divide 61 by 5, take $61 \times 2 = 122$ and make it 12.2.

How come this works? (Or doesn't it? Did I just pick two examples that happened to work?)

If a <u>polygon</u> is a multisided figure (like a triangle or a square, for instance), what do you think a <u>nonagon</u> is?

Reference

Algebra Word Problems— Diophantine Problems

Classroom Quickies, Books 1–3

DIOPHANTINE PROBLEM

PROBLEM

91. Claudine and her brother, Barry, are planning a party for their parents' twentieth wedding anniversary.

They figure they will need 100 pounds of meat, fish, and poultry for the buffet, but they have only $100 to spend on this.

They have priced boned chicken at 3 pounds for $2, rolled roast at 2 pounds for $7, and filleted salmon at $8 a pound.

How many whole pounds of each should they buy to get 100 pounds for $100?

MISCELLANEOUS PROBLEMS

PROBLEMS

92. When it is 2:00 A.M. in Los Angeles, it is 4:00 A.M. in Chicago and 5:00 A.M. in New York City.

It makes sense that Chicago is closer in time to New York City than to Los Angeles, since the distance from Chicago to New York City is less than half the distance from Chicago to Los Angeles.

It also makes sense that Chicago is closer in time to Los Angeles than New York City is, since Chicago is closer to Los Angeles than New York City is.

		Chicago *	New York City *
	Denver *		
Los Angeles *			
Pacific Time Zone	Mountain Time Zone	Central Time Zone	Eastern Time Zone

All right, now that you understand that, here's another bit of information.

When it is 2:00 A.M. in Los Angeles and 5:00 A.M. in New York City, then it is 8:00 P.M. (of that same day) in Sydney, Australia.

In other words, Sydney is 3 hours closer in time to New York City than it is to Los Angeles.

So how come Sydney isn't closer (in miles) to New York City than it is to Los Angeles? Or is it?

93.   Given four consecutive integers, prove

   a.   exactly two of the numbers have a factor of 2.

   b.   at least one of the numbers has a factor of 3.

   c.   no two of the numbers have any other common factor (except 1, which is a factor of every integer).

> When the animals were first named, why was a hippopotamus called a hippopotamus?

Reference

Classroom Quickies, Books 1–3

Rearrange Letters

DIRECTIONS

Use the letters at the top to fill in the chart so that words are formed and the sentence makes sense.

A shaded space in the chart shows the end of a word. Two shaded spaces together show the end of a sentence.

Except for the last line, the end of a line is not the end of a word unless there is a shaded space there.

When you have filled in the chart, answer the question asked.

PROBLEM

94.

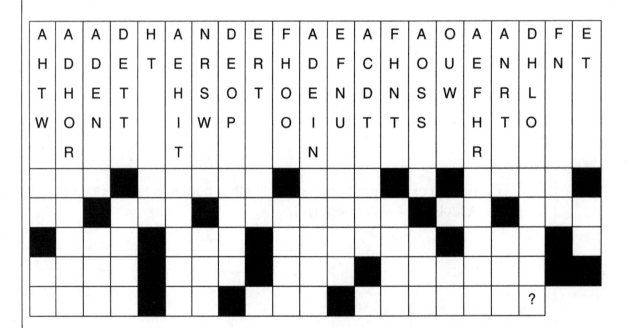

Reference

Basic Thinking Skills

FINDING COMMON ATTRIBUTES

DIRECTIONS

Each line contains four words.

Read all four words. They will all have something in common.

Decide what this common thing is, and write it down.

EXAMPLE

Problem: ball, wheel, plate, coin
Answer: round shape

PROBLEMS

95. rhombus, ellipse, pentagon, tetrahedron

96. short, brusque, abrupt, terse

97. Nash, Studebaker, Kaiser, Essex

98. arithmetic, algebra, geometry, trigonometry

99. eccentric, bizarre, oddball, peculiar

100. isosceles, scalene, equilateral, right

Reference

*Basic
Thinking
Skills*

IDENTIFYING THE OUTSIDER

DIRECTIONS

Read the five given terms.

Four of the terms have something in common.

The other term does not have this same quality.

Tell what the four terms have in common, and tell which term doesn't belong.

EXAMPLE

Problem: nice, big, mean, kind, nasty

Answer: ways to describe personality; big

PROBLEMS

101. addend, multiplier, subtrahend, divisor, product

102. London, Madrid, Oslo, Paris, Taipei

103. Spain, Mexico, Nicaragua, Canada, Brazil

104. caution, deer crossing, red light, stop, yield

105. fig, grape, squash, cucumber, watermelon

106. 2, 6, 9, 15, 24

Reference

*Basic
Thinking
Skills*

IDENTIFYING ANALOGOUS RELATIONSHIPS

DIRECTIONS

Each problem takes two lines. There are two terms on the first line. There are at least four terms on the second line.

On the first line, read the two terms and figure out how they are related. Then go to the second line and find this same relationship between the first term there and one of the remaining terms. Write the word you choose.

EXAMPLE

Problem: kind, unkind

nice, (big, hungry, nasty)

Answer: nasty

PROBLEMS

107. accountant, office

scientist, (computer, experiment, hospital, laboratory)

108. home run, baseball

strike, (baseball, football, bowling, ice hockey, wrestling)

109. 8 + 6, 14

8 − 6, (3/4, 4/3, 1, 2, 3, 6, 8)

110. 3 miles, 1760 yards

72 inches, (2 feet, 3 feet, 6 feet, 12 feet)

111. 5 ÷ 10, 2

24 ÷ 3, (8, 1/8, 1/2, 2, 6, 1/6)

Reference

*Basic
Thinking
Skills*

DIRECTIONS

Each problem takes two or three lines. Read the two terms on the first line and figure out how they are related. On the other lines are some **pairs** of terms. Choose the pair that are related in the same way as the terms on the first line.

EXAMPLE

Problem: hard, soft

(work, play / cement, mud / mud, steel)

Answer: cement, mud

PROBLEMS

112. cause, effect

(hungry, food / tape, music / lightning, thunder)

113. individual, clone

(human, android / fact, fiction / calculator, computer / original, copy)

114. praise, belittle

(laud, flatter / condemn, insult / compliment, criticize / blame, denigrate)

115. anticipate, fear

(surprise, nonchalance / hope, dread / interest, apathy / right, wrong)

116. anticipate, forethought

(retrospect, hindsight / smile, laugh / look for, find / predict, hope for)

117. felony, misdemeanor

(crime, infraction / stealing, looting / condemned, accused / major, minor)

Reference

Basic Thinking Skills

DIRECTIONS

Each problem is given in the form of a chart.

The words for the last two columns are listed (by column, in alphabetical order) below the chart.

Each line of the chart is a small problem by itself.

For each line, read the first two words and decide how they are related. Then find a third and fourth word (from the bottom) that are related in the same way.

EXAMPLE

Problem:

able	unable		
active	inactive		
ask	why		
fleas	dog		
quarter	1/4		

3rd column: alive, answer, can, half, lice
4th column: because, cannot, dead, human, 1/2

Answer:

able	unable	can	cannot
active	inactive	alive	dead
ask	why	answer	because
fleas	dog	lice	human
quarter	1/4	half	1/2

Reference

*Basic
Thinking
Skills*

PROBLEMS

118.

occupation	career		
year	light-year		
imply	infer		
original	reproduction		
infinite	finite		
triangle	circle		

Column 3: indicate, invention, recreation, tetrahedron, time, universe

Column 4: deduce, distance, galaxy, hobby, imitation, sphere

Reference

*Basic
Thinking
Skills*

119.

zoology	botany		
football	baseball		
common fund	kitty		
physician	veterinarian		
boil	broil		
gemstone	rock		
industrial	residential		

Column 3: animal, diamond, gridiron, human, plant, pool, pot

Column 4: animal, diamond, gridiron, house, plant, pot, shale

STATING ANALOGIES IN STANDARD FORM

LESSON

Suppose we find a relation between two things, and we find the same relation between two other things. Then we say there is an **analogous** (uh NAL uh gus) relationship between the two pairs.

EXAMPLE

There is an analogous relationship between the pair

>   hot   cold

and the pair

>   steam   ice

To state the analogy (uh NAL uh jee) between the two pairs, we will use the words "is to" and "as":

Hot is to **cold** as **steam** is to **ice**.

DIRECTIONS FOR PROBLEMS 120–24

Each problem takes two or three lines.

On the first line are a pair of terms. Figure out how they are related.

On the other lines are several pairs of terms. Choose the pair that are analogous to the pair on the first line.

Then state the analogy between the two pairs.

Example

Problem: hot, cold
>   (big, little / ice, steam / steam, ice / right, wrong)
Answer: Hot is to cold as steam is to ice.

PROBLEMS

120. hot, cold

>   (day, night / camel, polar bear / volcano, glacier / London, Moscow)

121. elephant, ant

(carnivore, herbivore / plains, forest / destructive, constructive / vertebrate, invertebrate)

122. radar, sonar

(civilian, military / air, water / receiver, transmitter / patrol car, airport)

123. acute, obtuse

(perceptive, insensitive / loyal, deceitful / risky, reliable / dangerous, innocuous)

124. hammer, saw

(cut, pound / force, persuasion / screwdriver, wrench / plumber, carpenter / batter, slice)

PROBLEM

125. Challenge

Use this list of words in two analogies, four words each with no repetition:

crucial, durable, ephemeral, important, permanent, picayune, transitory, trivial

REARRANGING ANALOGIES

LESSON

If we find an analogy between two pairs of things, we can rearrange the four things so that there are other analogies, too. For instance, with the two pairs

hot, cold / steam, ice

all of these would be correct:

Hot	is to	cold	as	steam	is to	ice.
Cold	is to	hot	as	ice	is to	steam.
Steam	is to	ice	as	hot	is to	cold.
Ice	is to	steam	as	cold	is to	hot.
Hot	is to	steam	as	cold	is to	ice.
Steam	is to	hot	as	ice	is to	cold.
Cold	is to	ice	as	hot	is to	steam.
Ice	is to	cold	as	steam	is to	hot.

Don't be fooled into thinking an analogy will be correct no matter how you position the terms. There are 24 ways to list 4 terms, and only 8 of these will work. Here are some of the 16 incorrect arrangements for the four terms above:

Hot	is to	cold	as	ice	is to	steam.
Hot	is to	ice	as	cold	is to	steam.
Steam	is to	ice	as	cold	is to	hot.
Cold	is to	ice	as	steam	is to	hot.

DIRECTIONS

You are given four terms. If they can be split into analogous pairs, list at least three correct analogies.

EXAMPLE

Problem: speaker, hear, talk, listener

Answer: (Any three of these would be correct.)

Speaker is to talk as listener is to hear.

Speaker is to listener as talk is to hear.

Hear is to listener as talk is to speaker.

Hear is to talk as listener is to speaker.

Talk is to speaker as hear is to listener.

Talk is to hear as speaker is to listener.

Listener is to speaker as hear is to talk.

Listener is to hear as speaker is to talk.

PROBLEMS

126.   typhoon, West Indies, Philippines, hurricane

127.   compliment, honesty, flattery, exaggeration

128.   complement, complete, enhance, supplement

129.   earthquake, tidal wave, sea, land

130.   theorem, conjecture, guesswork, proof

ANALOGIES

DIRECTIONS

This problem is just for fun.

Each one of the four entries is a term for an analogy. The terms are arranged in the right order for an analogy, but they may be disguised by terrible puns, misspellings, homonyms, misleading definitions, and other good things.

Figure out what the correct terms are, and write the analogy.

PROBLEM

131.

sightless seashoreer

Edinburgh girl that starts in the right direction

set tahhsittocS

recordless attempt without reason

Hint: You'd probably do better on the second clue if you were living in about 1800 (or even 1900).

DIRECTIONS

This problem is just for fun.

Each entry is a term for an analogy. The terms are arranged in the right order for an analogy, but they may be disguised by terrible puns, misspellings, homonyms, misleading definitions, and other good things.

Figure out what the correct terms are, and write the analogy.

PROBLEM

132.

slight

atmosphere following $_{case}$ symbolic hydrogen

doss before a cheer

more than one hefty short Bradley without a backer

Hint: This would have something to do with a sweeping tool, except that there's an "ing" that goes on the end, and the first letter needs to have a loop toward the left on the end of it when it's turned upside down.

DIRECTIONS

This problem is just for fun.

Each entry is a term for an analogy. The terms are arranged in the right order for an analogy, but they may be disguised by terrible puns, misspellings, homonyms, misleading definitions, and other good things.

Figure out what the correct terms are, and write the analogy.

PROBLEM

133.

retrogressive bus runs into used knocking down knocking down knocking down knocking down but sightless

cockney he unfettered if

able able 10 10 do

10 10 victory tdividingo a gnu do do

WARNING: This one is harder than the others, so you're getting a delicate hint this time. The hint may seem a bit difficult to grasp, but if I made it too forthright it's obvious that you wouldn't have anything left to figure out, so you'll just have do the best you can with it. I'd be lying if I told you that the hint is this: the analogy has nothing to do with computers.

REASONING BY ANALOGY

LESSON

When you reason by **analogy**, you think, "This situation is a lot like that other situation. Therefore, the same thing will be true now that was true then."

In other words, an **analogy** looks at two things and says, "They are alike in some ways. So they are also alike in these other ways."

Some analogies are good ones, and some are not.

EXAMPLE 1

When Ezra takes a test, he closes his eyes while he thinks of an answer. He finishes at least 15 minutes early, and he always gets good test grades. I want to get good test grades, so I'm going to close my eyes while I think of an answer, and I'm going to finish at least 15 minutes early.

The two things being compared are (1) what Ezra does when he takes a test and (2) what I will do when I take the same test. I notice two things that Ezra does and that I intend to do, so the situations are alike in at least two ways. I figure that they should also be alike in the test grades Ezra and I get.

This is a very poor analogy. Ezra's test grades depend on the answers he gives, not on whether or not he closes his eyes or finishes early. So the two situations are not enough alike to make my conclusion reasonable.

EXAMPLE 2

Ezra studies before a test and he always gets good test grades. I asked him how he knows what to study, and he told me. I'm as smart as Ezra is, so if I study before a test like Ezra does, I should get good test grades, too.

This is a good analogy. In a case like this, the situations are said to be analogous.

Reference

*Inductive
Thinking
Skills*

DIRECTIONS

You are told about an analogy someone has used.

Tell whether you think the analogy is pretty good, so-so, or poor, or whether you need more information in order to decide.

Whatever you answer, tell why.

PROBLEM

134.　Barbara and Shirley live next door to each other.

Both houses are the same size, have the same number of rooms, and have a basement.

Barbara figures that the heating bill for the two houses should be about the same, since both houses have gas furnaces.

Reference

*Inductive
Thinking
Skills*

DIRECTIONS

You are told about an analogy someone has used.

Tell whether you think the analogy is pretty good, so-so, or poor, or whether you need more information in order to decide.

Whatever you answer, tell why.

PROBLEM

135. There are many word-processing programs on the market. When you install such a program in a computer, you can type any kind of text—say, letters, term papers, or novels. The typed words appear on the monitor (screen) and can be edited before any printing is done. For example, words (and even whole sections) can be changed, moved, erased, or inserted. When you have finished, your printer will print the final text.

Last month Moira's parents installed a word-processing program in their home computer for their children to use for homework. The family spent hours studying the training manual, but they were exasperated because the program was complicated to use and they couldn't always find information they wanted and they couldn't get the program to do everything it should be able to do.

Moira, a tenth grader, was disappointed at not being able to use the program for her homework. However, she is glad she found out how annoying such a program can be to use, because she will use this knowledge in choosing her career. She had planned to be a legal secretary after graduating from high school, but a legal secretary uses a word-processing program, and Moira's recent experience has shown her that she does not want to do that.

Reference

*Inductive
Thinking
Skills*

DIRECTIONS

You are told about an analogy someone has used.

Tell whether you think the analogy is pretty good, so-so, or poor, or whether you need more information in order to decide.

Whatever you answer, tell why.

PROBLEM

136. Mr. Smith owns a large department store. He employs several executives and requires them to get his approval of almost every decision.

EXAMPLES

When the Personnel Director wants to advertise for help, she must show Mr. Smith the ad she intends to run.

When the buyer for the Women's Wear department goes on a buying trip, she is not allowed to place any orders until she returns and discusses her findings with Mr. Smith.

When the Cafeteria Head wants to add a new dish to the menu, he must first notify Mr. Smith.

When the Chief Accountant wants to redistribute the work load among his staff, Mr. Smith must be consulted first.

This requirement of Mr. Smith's is extremely irritating to his executives, for it shows lack of trust in their abilities to make intelligent decisions and it wastes hours of time.

One of the executives remarked sourly, "Why have a watchdog if you're going to do your own barking?"

Reference

Classroom Quickies, Books 1–3

WEIGHING PROBLEM

PROBLEM

137.   You have six balls, all of which look exactly the same.

Five of them weigh the same, but the sixth one is slightly lighter or heavier.

You have a balance scale. How can you find the odd ball in at most three weighings?

REARRANGE LETTERS

DIRECTIONS

Use the letters at the top to fill in the chart so that words are formed and the sentence makes sense.

A shaded space in the chart shows the end of a word. Two shaded spaces together show the end of a sentence.

Except for the last line, the end of a line is not the end of a word unless there is a shaded space there.

When you have filled in the chart, answer the question asked.

PROBLEM

138.

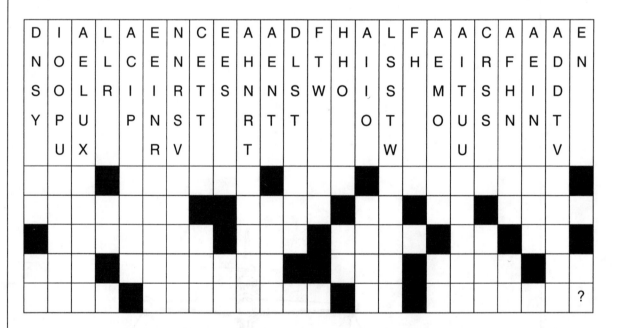

Reference

Classroom Quickies, Book 3

MISCELLANEOUS PROBLEM

PROBLEM

139. If you buy a set of computer games for $20 and sell them for $30 and then buy them back again for $40 and then sell them again for $50, how much money did you gain or lose all together on these deals?

> Did you know that Georgia was the fourth state to be admitted to the Union, coming only after Delaware (first), Pennsylvania (second), and New Jersey (third)?

DIOPHANTINE PROBLEM

PROBLEM

140. Barry and Claudine weren't satisfied with the prices they were quoted, because they'd have had to buy too much chicken and not enough beef and fish, so they went to another store.

This time, they were quoted prices of $3 for 5 pounds of boned chicken, $10 for 3 pounds of rolled roast, and $3 a pound for filleted pollock.

How many whole pounds of each should they buy in order to get 100 pounds for $100?

Old computer programmers never die. They just lose their memories.

FOLLOWING DIRECTIONS

DIRECTIONS

Take a sheet of paper and a pencil (or pen). Each part of the problem tells you to do something. Do it all on the same sheet of paper.

PROBLEM

141. a. Print your name in the upper right corner.

        b. Do part **c** near the top. For the rest of the problem, print each new result under the previous result.

        c. Print

IAMSOBRILLIANTTHAT

        d. If a twin pair of consonants is from the first half of the alphabet, replace the pair with "ME." If a twin pair of consonants is from the last half of the alphabet, replace the pair with "EM."

        e. Remove the first two and the last two letters.

        f. Leave the second consonant where it is, but insert a copy of it before and after the fourth vowel and between the last two consonants.

        g. Exchange the first and third consonants. Move the fourth consonant so that it replaces the fourth consonant from the right end.

        h. Make two copies of the third vowel. Insert one after the third consonant and the other at the right end.

        i. Change the first and last consonants to "L" and "F," respectively, and move them to the right end.

        j. Insert "T" between the second and third vowels, "C" just before the third vowel from the right end, and "Y" between the third and fourth consonants from the right end.

Reference

Basic Thinking Skills

MISCELLANEOUS PROBLEMS

PROBLEMS

142. A drawer has exactly 20 socks in it, of which 10 are white and 10 are black.

The socks are not sorted either by color or by pairs. They are, in fact, thoroughly mixed up.

Someone blindfolds you and tells you to start taking socks out of the drawer. You are not allowed to look and see what color you've taken.

a. What is the greatest number of socks you'd have to take out of the drawer in order to make sure that you had at least two of the same color?

(You don't care <u>which</u> color, as long as both are the same color.) Explain your answer.

b. Same as part **a**, except suppose that the drawer has 10 socks of each of three different colors.

c. Same as part **a** again, but this time suppose that the drawer has 10 socks of each of four different colors.

d. Same as part **a** again, but suppose the drawer has 10 socks of each of n different colors, where n is some specific number.

Reference

Basic
Thinking
Skills

143. When a telephone rings there are five seconds between the start of one ring and the start of the next ring. The ring itself lasts about a second.

Suppose you call someone and let the phone ring five times before hanging up.

How much time to answer the phone have you given the person you called?

144. You are staying with an English duke and duchess in their huge centuries-old stately home.

You have been told that a ghost floats by every four days and a skeleton rattles along every three weeks.

Suppose both a ghost floated by and a skeleton rattled along today.

How long will it be before a floating ghost and a rattling skeleton appear on the same day again?

Reference

Taken from

Basic Thinking Skills

THE TRUTH-TELLERS AND THE LIARS

> The people on a certain island are divided into two groups—the truth-tellers, and the liars.
>
> The truth-tellers always tell the truth.
>
> The liars always lie.
>
> There are no half-truths or half-lies.
>
> A stranger comes to the island one day and sees three of the natives standing together.

PROBLEMS 145–48

145. The first native says, "I am not a liar." The second native says, "He's lying." The third native says, "They're both lying."

What is the third native—a truth-teller, or a liar? Explain your answer.

146. The stranger asks one of the natives whether or not he is a liar. The native, a timid man, whispers his answer, and the stranger doesn't hear him. The second native says, "He said he's a liar, and he is."

a. Is the first native a truth-teller, or a liar? Explain.

b. Is the second native a truth-teller, or a liar? How do you know?

Reference

Taken
from

*Basic
Thinking
Skills*

147. The three natives are standing by a fork in the road. The stranger asks where the two branches of the road lead.

The first native says they both lead to the village.

The second native says they both lead to the jungle.

The third native says that one leads to the village and the other leads to the jungle.

Since the entire island is made up either of jungle or the village, the stranger knows that one of the natives has to be telling the truth. And since the statements are all mutually contradictory, two of the natives have to be lying.

So which native is telling the truth, and which two are liars, and how do you know?

Reference

*Basic
Thinking
Skills*

148. After being there for a few days, the stranger goes for a walk without paying attention to the way the road branches.

He comes to a fork in the road and knows that one way leads to the village, while the other way leads to the jungle.

A native is standing there, but the stranger doesn't know whether the native is a truth-teller, or a liar.

The stranger has made such a nuisance of himself by asking so many questions that he has been forbidden by the native leader to address more than one question a day to any one native.

What one question can the stranger ask the native so that the answer will tell him which branch of the road to take in order to get back to the village?

A newborn baby elephant weighs about 200 pounds and is about 3 feet tall.

ANALOGIES IN PROPORTIONS

LESSON

A fraction is a **ratio** (RAY sho).

A <u>true</u> statement that two ratios are equal is a **proportion** (pruh POR shun).

We say that two equal ratios are **in proportion** to each other or that they are **proportional**.

EXAMPLES 1

These are ratios:

$$\frac{1}{2} \qquad\qquad \frac{5}{3} \qquad\qquad \frac{243}{5716} \qquad\qquad \frac{5716}{243}$$

These are proportions:

$$\frac{1}{2} = \frac{3}{6} \qquad\qquad \frac{2}{1} = \frac{6}{3} \qquad\qquad \frac{48}{150} = \frac{8}{25}$$

These are proportional, and they are in proportion (to each other):

$$\frac{2}{1} \text{ and } \frac{10}{5} \qquad\qquad\qquad \frac{3}{5} \text{ and } \frac{6}{10}$$

To show that two ratios do NOT form a proportion, we strike a bar slantwise (/) through the equals sign (=) and get ≠.

EXAMPLES 2

It is false to say $\frac{1}{2} = \frac{2}{3}$, so instead we write $\frac{1}{2} \neq \frac{2}{3}$.

$\frac{1}{3}$ is **NOT** in proportion to $\frac{2}{3}$, so $\frac{1}{3} \neq \frac{2}{3}$.

$\frac{2}{3}$ is **NOT** proportional to $\frac{2}{5}$, so $\frac{2}{3} \neq \frac{2}{5}$.

These pairs of ratios are shown to be nonproportional:

$$\frac{1}{2} \neq \frac{2}{6} \qquad\qquad \frac{2}{1} \neq \frac{6}{4} \qquad\qquad \frac{48}{150} \neq \frac{8}{21}$$

A proportion can be stated as an analogy.

EXAMPLES 3

$\frac{1}{2} = \frac{3}{6}$, so 1 is to 2 as 3 is to 6.

$\frac{48}{150} = \frac{8}{25}$, so 48 is to 150 as 8 is to 25.

Notice that an analogy uses "is to" instead of a fraction bar (—) and uses "as" instead of an equals sign (=). So, given the proportion

$$\frac{2}{4} = \frac{5}{10},$$

an analogy reads it as

2 is to 4 as 5 is to 10

instead of

two fourths equals five tenths

and instead of

2 divided by 4 equals 5 divided by 10.

If two ratios are nonproportional, an analogy cannot be formed from them. Conversely, if an analogy cannot be formed from two ratios, then the ratios are not proportional.

EXAMPLES 4

$\frac{1}{2} \neq \frac{3}{5}$, so it is false that 1 is to 2 as 3 is to 5.

It is not true that 2 is to 3 as 4 is to 7, so $\frac{2}{3} \neq \frac{4}{7}$.

DIRECTIONS

You are given four numbers. Tell whether or not they can be used to form a proportion.

If they can, then use them to write at least three different proportions. Also state each proportion as an analogy.

EXAMPLE 1

Problem: 4, 5, 2, 10

Answer: Yes.

$\frac{4}{2} = \frac{10}{5}$;   4 is to 2 as 10 is to 5

$\frac{2}{5} = \frac{4}{10}$;   2 is to 5 as 4 is to 10

$\frac{2}{4} = \frac{5}{10}$;   2 is to 4 as 5 is to 10

(There are also five other proportions that can be made from these four numbers.)

EXAMPLE 2

Problem: 1, 5, 2, 8

Answer: No.

PROBLEMS

149.   2, 15, 5, 6

150.   3, 24, 2, 8

151.   8, 12, 6, 16

152.   8, 36, 48, 6

153.   4, 12, 6, 16

154.   1/2, 2/3, 8, 6

PROPORTIONS

HINTS FOR PROBLEMS ON PAGES 95–108

If a problem talks about a common factor, assume that this factor is not 1. Also assume that all numbers are greater than zero.

If you are not given any numbers, find numbers of your own to use. See how they relate to each other or what happens to them when you do what the problem says.

Then choose another set of numbers. See if they relate to each other or act in the same way as the first numbers did.

Keep choosing numbers until you can <u>predict</u> what they have to be like, or what will happen to them in the problem. (Or maybe you feel that <u>no</u> numbers will work.) Figure out how to prove that your reasoning would apply no matter which (allowable) numbers were chosen.

You are allowed to use anything already proved. For example, if you are doing problem 164 and need to use a statement proved in problem 160, then you may do so without proving it again.

To help yourself imagine a general proportion, make a set of fraction bars and an equals sign

$$\rule{2cm}{0.4pt} \quad = \quad \rule{2cm}{0.4pt}$$

and fill in the four terms with four different geometric figures—say, a circle, a square, a triangle, and a rhombus:

$$\frac{\bigcirc}{\square} = \frac{\triangle}{\diagup\!\!\!\!\diagdown}$$

Then you'll have something to stare at while you're trying to figure out how to solve the problem.

155. You are given a proportion. Prove:

a. If the numerators are equal, then the denominators are equal.

b. If the denominators are equal, then the numerators are equal.

c. Even if you hadn't been told at the start of this series of problems that all numbers would be nonzero, the denominators would still have to be nonzero.

Here is what was proved in problem 155. (GAP = Given a proportion.)

155.   GAP, if the numerators are =, then the denominators are =, and vice versa.

LESSON

A proportion always looks like this:

$$\frac{\text{first term}}{\text{second term}} = \frac{\text{third term}}{\text{fourth term}}$$

The first and fourth terms are called the **extremes**, or the outer terms, of the proportion.

The second and third terms are called the **means**, or the inner terms, of the proportion.

PROBLEM

156.   You are given a proportion.

Prove that the product of the extremes equals the product of the means.

Note: Here are two other ways to state what you are to prove.

first term × fourth term = second term × third term

product of outer terms = product of inner terms

Here is a list of the two problems proved so far. In this list, GAP = Given a proportion.

155. GAP, if the numerators are =, then the denominators are =, and vice versa.

156. GAP, the product of the extremes = the product of the means.

LESSON

If you can understand how an **indirect proof** works, you will have a powerful mathematical tool available for use. The steps for an indirect proof are these:

1) Take the <u>opposite</u> of what is to be proved, and suppose it is true.

2) Follow through until a contradiction is reached.

3) Conclude that the supposition has to be wrong.

EXAMPLE

Problem:

Prove that if one ratio in a proportion has a value of 1, then the other ratio also has a value of 1.

(Indirect) Proof:

Suppose the second ratio is not worth 1. Then the two ratios are unequal, and so they cannot be proportional. This is a contradiction, because we are given a proportion. Therefore, our supposition has to be wrong, and so the second ratio has a value of 1.

Now try using an indirect proof on the problem below.

PROBLEM

157. Prove that if a ratio has two unequal terms, and if another ratio is in proportion to it, then the terms of the second ratio are also unequal.

Here is a list of some of the problems proved. In this list, GAP = Given a proportion.

155. GAP, if the numerators are =, then the denominators are =, and vice versa.

156. GAP, the product of the extremes = the product of the means.

158. You are given that the product of two numbers equals the product of two other numbers. (For example, $3 \times 4 = 2 \times 6$.)

Prove that a proportion will be formed if you use one pair of numbers as the extremes and you use the other pair as the means. While you're at it, prove that

a. it doesn't matter which pair you choose for the extremes;

b. the numbers in the pair you choose can be used in either order;

c. the numbers in the other pair can be used in either order; and

d. any of the four given numbers can be used as the first term.

EXAMPLE

Given $3 \times 4 = 2 \times 6$.

Suppose you choose 2 and 6 to be the extremes. Then either 2 or 6 can be the first term, and the other number will be the fourth term.

This has left 3 and 4 to be the means. Either 3 or 4 can be the second term, and the other number will be the third term.

Hint: You are given an equation. Remember that both sides of an equation can be divided by the same number.

Here is a list of some of the problems proved. In this list, # = number; GAP = Given a proportion.

155. GAP, if the numerators are =, then the denominators are =, and vice versa.

156. GAP, the product of the extremes = the product of the means.

158. If you have = products of two pairs of #s, then either pair can be the extremes of a proportion, and the other pair will be the means. The #s in a pair may be used in either order, and any term may be chosen as the first term.

159. You are given a proportion.

Prove that you will still have a proportion if you switch (with each other)

a. the means of the given proportion.

b. the extremes of the given proportion.

Note: The new proportions will be different from the old proportion.

Here is a list of some problems proved. If you're told you can do something to a proportion, then you will still have a proportion afterwards. In this list, # = number; GAP = Given a proportion.

155. GAP, if the numerators are =, then the denominators are =, and vice versa.

156. GAP, the product of the extremes = the product of the means.

158. If you have = products of two pairs of #s, then either pair can be the extremes of a proportion, and the other pair will be the means. The #s in a pair may be used in either order, and any term may be chosen as the first term.

159. GAP, the means can be switched, and so can the extremes.

160. You are given a proportion.

Prove that if you invert both of the proportion's ratios, the result will still be a proportion.

Here is a list of some problems proved. If you're told you can do something to a proportion, then you will still have a proportion afterwards. In this list, # = number; GAP = Given a proportion.

156. GAP, the product of the extremes = the product of the means.

158. If you have = products of two pairs of #s, then either pair can be the extremes of a proportion, and the other pair will be the means. The #s in a pair may be used in either order, and any term may be chosen as the first term.

160. GAP, the ratios can be inverted.

161. You are given a proportion. You keep the same denominators, but you add to each ratio's numerator the amount of that ratio's denominator.

EXAMPLE

Given $\frac{2}{5} = \frac{6}{15}$, you make it $\frac{2+5}{5} = \frac{6+15}{15}$, or $\frac{7}{5} = \frac{21}{15}$.

Prove that the new ratios are proportional.

Hint: Add 1 to each side of the equation.

Note: When this appears in a problem list (at the top of a page), it will be abbreviated as: GAP, numerators may be increased by denominators.

Here is a list of some problems proved. If you're told you can do something to a proportion, then you will still have a proportion afterwards. In this list, # = number; GAP = Given a proportion.

155. GAP, if the numerators are =, then the denominators are =, and vice versa.

156. GAP, the product of the extremes = the product of the means.

158. If you have = products of two pairs of #s, then either pair can be the extremes of a proportion, and the other pair will be the means. The #s in a pair may be used in either order, and any term may be chosen as the first term.

159. GAP, the means can be switched, and so can the extremes.

160. GAP, the ratios can be inverted.

161. GAP, numerators may be increased by denominators.

162. You are given four numbers that will be terms of a proportion if you can place them correctly.

Prove that a proportion can be formed no matter which one of the four numbers you use as the first term, if

a. two of the numbers are the same, and the other two numbers are different from each other and from the first two.

b. the four numbers are distinct.

Here is a list of some problems proved. If you're told you can do something to a proportion, then you will still have a proportion afterwards. In this list, # = number; GAP = Given a proportion.

161. GAP, numerators may be increased by denominators.

162. Given four #s that can be terms of a proportion, any of them can be chosen as the first term.

163. You are given four distinct whole numbers, none of which is 1, and are told to organize them into a proportion.

a. Can this possibly be done if three of the numbers have a common factor but the other number does not have this factor?

If so, give an example of such a proportion. If not, explain why not.

b. Suppose no two of these numbers have a common factor.

Prove that it is not possible to use the numbers to form a proportion.

Hint for part **b**: Try an indirect proof here. (Suppose that it <u>is</u> possible to use the numbers to form a proportion, and see what happens.)

c. Suppose that all four numbers have a common factor, and suppose you divide this common factor out of all four numbers, leaving four new numbers.

Prove: If your new numbers

1) can form a proportion, then the original numbers can form a proportion, too.

2) cannot form a proportion, then the original numbers cannot form a proportion, either.

Hint for part **c(2)**: Try an indirect proof here.

Here is a list of some problems proved. If you're told you can do something to a proportion, then you will still have a proportion afterwards. In this list, # = number; GAP = Given a proportion.

155. GAP, if the numerators are =, then the denominators are =, and vice versa.

156. GAP, the product of the extremes = the product of the means.

158. If you have = products of two pairs of #s, then either pair can be the extremes of a proportion, and the other pair will be the means. The #s in a pair may be used in either order, and any term may be chosen as the first term.

159. GAP, the means can be switched, and so can the extremes.

160. GAP, the ratios can be inverted.

161. GAP, numerators may be increased by denominators.

162. Given four #s that can be terms of a proportion, any of them can be chosen as the first term.

163. Given four #s, if no two have a common factor, then the #s cannot be the terms of a proportion.

164. You are given four numbers that can be arranged to form a proportion.

Prove that you can start the arrangement by choosing any one of the four numbers for any one of the four terms of a proportion.

Here is a list of some problems proved. If you're told you can do something to a proportion, then you will still have a proportion afterwards. In this list, # = number; GAP = Given a proportion.

156. GAP, the product of the extremes = the product of the means.

159. GAP, the means can be switched, and so can the extremes.

160. GAP, the ratios can be inverted.

161. GAP, numerators may be increased by denominators.

162. Given four #s that can be terms of a proportion, any of them can be chosen as the first term.

163. Given four #s, if no two have a common factor, then the #s cannot be the terms of a proportion.

165. You are given four numbers and you don't know whether or not they can be positioned to form a proportion.

Prove:

a. If you choose a number as the first term, then you need try at most only two of the three remaining numbers as the second term in order to decide whether or not a proportion can be formed.

b. If you don't get a proportion from part **a** above, then a proportion can't be formed even if you choose a different first term.

Here is a list of some problems proved. If you're told you can do something to a proportion, then you will still have a proportion afterwards. In this list, # = number; GAP = Given a proportion.

156. GAP, the product of the extremes = the product of the means.

159. GAP, the means can be switched, and so can the extremes.

160. GAP, the ratios can be inverted.

164. Given four #s that can form a proportion, any number chosen first can be used for any of the four terms.

165. Given that you've chosen one of four #s as the first term of a potential proportion, if two of the remaining three #s don't work as a second term, then a proportion can't be formed.

166. You have four numbers and decide to see if they can form a proportion.

You choose two of them—one for the first term and one for the second term.

You use the other two numbers as the third and fourth terms, but you don't get a proportion.

You switch the last two terms and still don't get a proportion.

a. Might you get a proportion if you switch the first and second terms? If so, give an example of such a case. If not, tell why not.

b. You intend to try again, so you keep the same first term, but you choose a different second term.

   1) Is that really necessary? (You didn't get a proportion using the number you first chose as the second term, so wasn't that enough to show that the four numbers will not form a proportion?) Explain.

   2) If you think you should try a different second term, what if this one doesn't work, either? You will have tested two of the three numbers available. Will that last number have to be tested, too? Explain.

c. Could your answers to the questions above change if you happened to choose a different one of the given numbers as the first term? Explain.

Here is a list of some problems proved. If you're told you can do something to a proportion, then you will still have a proportion afterwards. In this list, # = number; GAP = Given a proportion.

156. GAP, the product of the extremes = the product of the means.

158. If you have = products of two pairs of #s, then either pair can be the extremes of a proportion, and the other pair will be the means. The #s in a pair may be used in either order, and any term may be chosen as the first term.

159. GAP, the means can be switched, and so can the extremes.

160. GAP, the ratios can be inverted.

161. GAP, numerators may be increased by denominators.

164. Given four #s that can form a proportion, any # chosen first can be used for any of the four terms.

165. Given that you've chosen one of four #s as the first term of a potential proportion, if two of the remaining three #s don't work as a second term, then a proportion can't be formed.

167. The numbers 1, 2, 3, and 4 cannot be used to form a proportion, no matter in what order they are used. (Try it and see. For all you know, I may be lying to you.)

Is there <u>any</u> set of four consecutive numbers that can be used to form a proportion?

If so, what are they, and what is the proportion?

If not, prove it.

Here is a list of some problems proved. If you're told you can do something to a proportion, then you will still have a proportion afterwards. In this list, # = number; GAP = Given a proportion.

156. GAP, the product of the extremes = the product of the means.

158. If you have = products of two pairs of #s, then either pair can be the extremes of a proportion, and the other pair will be the means. The #s in a pair may be used in either order, and any term may be chosen as the first term.

160. GAP, the ratios can be inverted.

161. GAP, numerators may be increased by denominators.

168. You are given a proportion.

You leave the right-hand ratio alone, but you add its numerator to the left-hand ratio's numerator, and you add its denominator to the left-hand ratio's denominator.

EXAMPLE

Given $\frac{2}{3} = \frac{4}{6}$, you make it $\frac{2+4}{3+6} = \frac{4}{6}$, or $\frac{6}{9} = \frac{4}{6}$.

In the example above, you still have a proportion, but will you always have a proportion no matter what numbers you start with?

Prove your answer.

MISCELLANEOUS PROBLEMS

DIRECTIONS

Assume that the bricklayers are all equally efficient and that they work at a set pace whether working alone or with another bricklayer.

Also assume that if two or more bricklayers work together on a job, the amount accomplished is the sum of what each one accomplishes. For example, assume that if two bricklayers work together for a month, they do the same amount of work as either one of them would do in two months.

PROBLEM

169. If four bricklayers can do four jobs in four days,

    a. how long will it take eight bricklayers to do eight jobs?

    b. how many jobs can eight bricklayers do in eight days?

    c. how many bricklayers does it take to do eight jobs in eight days?

    d. how many bricklayers will it take to do ten jobs in ten days?

    e. how many jobs can four bricklayers do in six days?

Reference

Classroom Quickies, Books 1–3

WATER JUGS PROBLEM

PROBLEM

170. You have 3 water jugs.

They hold, respectively, 4, 9, and 12 quarts.

They are unmarked, so you can't tell how much water is in them just by looking at them (unless they are full).

The 12-quart jug is full. There is no other water supply.

Tell how you can get two measures of exactly 6 quarts each.

MISCELLANEOUS PROBLEM

PROBLEM

171. The number of hairs on the human head can be anywhere from 0 through 200,000.

Prove that at least ten people in New York City have exactly the same number of hairs on their heads (as each other).

Reference

*Algebra
Word
Problems—
Diophantine
Problems*

*Classroom
Quickies,
Books 1–
3*

DIOPHANTINE PROBLEM

PROBLEM

172. Claudine and Barry still weren't happy about having to offer so much more chicken than beef or fish, but they thought they probably wouldn't get better prices quoted on either the chicken or the fish.

With the thought of making Swiss steak instead of rolled roast for the buffet, they asked the price of boneless round steak and were told $5 for 2 pounds.

The prices they had been quoted then were: boned chicken, $3 for 5 pounds; boneless round steak, $5 for 2 pounds; filleted pollock, $3 a pound.

How many whole pounds of each can they get if they buy 100 pounds for $100?

> If we call a horse's tail a leg, then how many legs does a horse have?

MISCELLANEOUS PROBLEMS

PROBLEMS

173. Pasquale had more problems right on today's test than Neil had right on yesterday's test.

Marnie had more problems right on yesterday's test than Pasquale had right on today's test.

Did Marnie have a higher percentage of problems right on yesterday's test than

a. Neil had?

b. Pasquale had on today's test?

174. Abner had a higher percentage of problems right on today's test than Brenda had on yesterday's test.

Norma had a higher percentage of problems right on yesterday's test than Abner had on today's test.

a. Did Abner have more problems right on today's test than Brenda had right on yesterday's test?

b–d. On yesterday's test, did Norma have

b. a higher percentage of problems right than Brenda had?

c. more problems right than Brenda had?

d. more problems right than Abner had right on today's test?

Reference

Classroom Quickies, Books 1–3

REARRANGE LETTERS

DIRECTIONS

Use the letters at the top to fill in the chart so that words are formed and the sentence makes sense.

A shaded space in the chart shows the end of a word. Two shaded spaces together show the end of a sentence.

Except for the last line, the end of a line is not the end of a word unless there is a shaded space there.

When you have filled in the chart, answer the question asked.

PROBLEM

175.

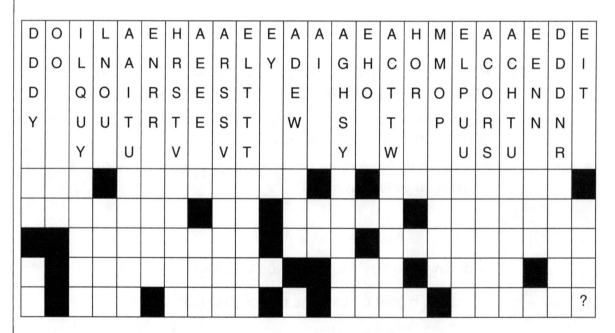

WEIGHING PROBLEM

PROBLEM

176. You are given a balance scale and one each of weights of 1, 3, 9, 27, and 81 pounds.

Explain how you can weigh any object from 1 through 121 pounds.

(You may assume that either you have a large scale or will weigh only small objects so that fitting the object into one of the pans will not be a problem.)

You must use only the five given weights. You are not allowed to find the weight of, say a 3-pound radio, and then use the radio along with the 3-pound and 9-pound weights to weigh a 15-pound box of tools.

When you have solved that problem, try this one:

Suppose you wanted to be able to weigh objects heavier than 121 pounds.

What is the next size of weight you'd need, and what is the heaviest object you'd then be able to weigh?

Reference

*Math
Word
Problems*

MISCELLANEOUS PROBLEMS

DIRECTIONS

When we are served by a waiter or waitress, it is customary to leave a tip for about 15% of the bill.

It isn't always possible to leave 15%. For example, 15% of $1.25 is $18\frac{3}{4}$¢, so the closest we could get would be 19¢. But we don't want to start counting out pennies, either, so we'll say to leave a tip to the nearest nickel, 20¢ in this case.

Tell how much should be left for a tip if the bill is for the amount shown. Give two answers for each problem—the first to the nearest nickel, and the second to the next higher nickel if the answer doesn't come out on a nickel.

EXAMPLES

If your percentage answer comes out to 17.25¢, your answers will be 15¢ and 20¢.

If your percentage answer comes out to $17\frac{1}{2}$¢, both answers will be 20¢.

If your percentage answer comes out to 20¢, both answers will be 20¢.

PROBLEM

177. a. $2.00

b. $2.50

c. $1.10

d. $3.75

e. $8.50

Reference

Math
Word
Problems

AREAS

DIRECTIONS FOR PROBLEM 178

All tiles are square. When tiling the floor, you may not put two pieces of tile together to make a wider piece of tile.

For example, if you have a 2 in. × 12 in. strip of tile and a 4 in. × 12 in. strip of tile, you are not allowed to lay them together to make a 6 in. × 12 in. strip. (However, you are allowed to cut the 4 in. × 12 in. strip into two 2 in. × 12 in. strips and then lay the three strips end to end to form a strip 2 in. × 36 in.)

Keep track of your answers, because you'll need them to answer the problems on the next page. (If you don't mind doing all the work again, you can ignore this direction.)

178. A. Give your answer in both sq in. and sq ft.

What is the area of a tile if a side of it measures

a. 12 in.?

b. 9 in.?

B–C. You can buy single tiles but not a part of a tile.

B. How many tiles should you buy to cover a 12 ft × 15 ft floor if a side of a tile measures

a. 12 in.?

b. 9 in.?

C. How many tiles should you buy to cover an 11 ft × 11 ft floor if a side of a tile measures

a. 12 in.?

b. 9 in.?

[Problem continued on next page.]

Reference

*Math
Word
Problems*

[Problem continued from previous page.]

D. Suppose you can't buy the tiles individually but have to buy them in boxes of a dozen each.

Then how many <u>boxes</u> of tiles should you buy to cover a floor

a. 12 ft × 15 ft if the tiles are 12-in. squares?

b. 12 ft × 15 ft if the tiles are 9-in. squares?

c. 11 ft × 11 ft if the tiles are 12-in. squares?

d. 11 ft × 11 ft if the tiles are 9-in. squares?

E. Keep track of your answers to this one for the problem on the next page.

Suppose you have to buy the tiles in boxes of 20 each at $25 a box.

Then how many boxes of tiles should you buy, and what will the cost of the tiles be, to cover a floor

a. 12 ft × 15 ft if the tiles are 12-in. squares?

b. 12 ft × 15 ft if the tiles are 9-in. squares?

c. 11 ft × 11 ft if the tiles are 12-in. squares?

d. 11 ft × 11 ft if the tiles are 9-in. squares?

[Problem continued on next page.]

Reference

*Math
Word
Problems*

[Problem continued from previous page.]

F. You still have to buy the tiles in boxes of 20 each at $25 a box, but if the total comes to $310 or more, you get a 10% discount on the whole purchase.

Now how many boxes of tiles should you buy, and what will the cost of the tiles be, to cover a floor

a. 12 ft × 15 ft if the tiles are 12-in. squares?

b. 12 ft × 15 ft if the tiles are 9-in. squares?

c. 11 ft × 11 ft if the tiles are 12-in. squares?

d. 11 ft × 11 ft if the tiles are 9-in. squares?

PROBLEM

179. You have a square whose sides are each 6 inches long.

Both diagonals are drawn.

What is the area of each of the four triangles whose vertices meet at the intersection of the diagonals?

Reference

Taken from

Mind Benders®— B3

MIND BENDERS®

PROBLEMS

180. Four married couples (Edgewoods, Framptons, Learneds, MacArthurs) each have an old car (Hudson, Kaiser, Packard, Studebaker) for the first time. The wives' first names are Anne, Cheryl, Jessica, and Nora. The husbands' first names are Bertram, Douglas, Gino, and Rex.

Match up everything from the clues below.

Note: Read carefully. If a clue says something like, "John and Mary talked about their car," then you have two people and one car, so John and Mary must be married. But if it says "cars" instead of "car," then John and Mary must not be married, since each couple have only one old car.

1.   The Edgewoods, who do not have the Kaiser, asked Nora how she found her old car.

2.   Neither Jessica and her husband nor the Learneds have the Packard or the Studebaker.

3.   Gino and his wife, who don't own the Hudson, asked Cheryl and her husband if they thought the MacArthurs and the owners of the Studebaker would like to join the four of them for dinner.

4.   The Framptons went to a baseball game with Rex and Bertram and their wives.

5.   Jessica and Douglas were discussing how much their cars are worth, when the Hudson owners came along and suggested they all take their cars to an appraiser.

6.   Gino and his wife are not the Framptons.

7.   Bertram and his wife don't have the Kaiser.

Reference

Taken from

Mind Benders®—B3

Chart for problem 180

	Bertram	Douglas	Gino	Rex	Edge-wood	Frampton	Learned	MacArthur	Hudson	Kaiser	Packard	Stude-baker
Anne												
Cheryl												
Jessica												
Nora												
Edge-wood												
Frampton												
Learned												
MacArthur												
Hudson												
Kaiser												
Packard												
Stude-baker												

Reference

Taken
from

*Mind
Benders®—
C3*

181. Six space ship captains (three men, three women), whose names are Jakar, Kaliz, Otphor, Telerp, Umnak, and Zadok, come from different solar systems (suns are Arcturus, Capella, Deneb, Procyon, Sirius, Vega), have different enemies (Xabot, Xenn, Xighu, Xorbus, Xulloc, Xydan), and different defensive weapons (electroray, force field, gravitron, hyperscope, magnetor, neutronom). Each solar system contains a different number of planets (9, 10, 11, 13, 16, 20), and the sky of each person's home planet is a different color (blue, ivory, lavender, rose, white, yellow).

Find each person's name, sex, sun, sky color, sun's number of planets, enemy, and weapon.

1. Kaliz' sun has more planets than the sun of Xabot's enemy, but it has fewer planets than the electroray user's sun.

2. The women whose planets have the yellow sky and the white sky do not use the gravitron.

3. The person whose sun has 11 planets does not use the hyperscope and she doesn't have Xydan for an enemy.

4. The force field user likes his weapon better than the others, but the Vegan thinks his own weapon is superior to the force field.

5. Otphor's ship is the same color as the sky of his home planet, which is not lavender.

6. Zadok's enemy, who is not Xabot, nearly got the better of him last month.

7. Even though he was cheered on from the sidelines by the man whose enemy is Xighu, Jakar lost a race with the Vegan.

8. The man from Arcturus is a good friend of Zadok, whose home planet does not have the blue sky.

9. Otphor's sun has more planets than the suns of Xorbus' enemy and the planet with the blue sky, but it has fewer planets than Sirius and the sun of Umnak.

10. Xabot's enemy, who graduated at the top of his class, is neither the man from Capella nor the force field user.

11. The planet with the white sky is not in the solar system which has 16 planets.

12. Xulloc is not the enemy of Kaliz or Telerp.

13. The sun of Xighu's enemy has more planets than the sun which has the planet with the rose sky.

14. Procyon has fewer planets than the sun of the gravitron user but has more planets than the magnetor user's sun.

Reference

Taken from

Mind Benders®— C3

Chart for problem 181

	Arcturus	Capella	Deneb	Procyon	Sirius	Vega	blue	ivory	lavender	rose	white	yellow	9	10	11	13	16	20	Xabot	Xenn	Xighu	Xorbus	Xulloc	Xydan	electroray	force field	gravitron	hyperscope	magnetor	neutronom
Jakar																														
Kaliz																														
Otphor																															
Telerp																															
Umnak																															
Zadok																															
blue																															
ivory																															
lavender																															
rose																															
white																															
yellow																															
9																															
10																															
11																															
13																															
16																															
20																															
Xabot																															
Xenn																															
Xighu																															
Xorbus																															
Xulloc																															
Xydan																															
electroray																															
force field																															
gravitron																															
hyperscope																															
magnetor																															
neutronom																															

Reference

Math Mind Benders®— Warm Up

MATH MIND BENDERS®

LESSON

Your answers will be numbers. An answer might have one or more digits. Only one digit of an answer goes in a square.

Some of the squares in the grid are numbered so that they may be easily named.

"1-A" means that the answer starts in square 1 and reads across.

"4-D" means that the answer starts in square 4 and reads down.

1-A is a two-digit answer. (In the second grid 1-A is 47.) Two-digit answers also go in 1-D (45), 4-D (12), and 5-A (32).

One-digit answers go in 2-D (7), 3-A (5), 4-A (1), and 5-D (3).

As you can see, this kind of grid will take eight answers.

1	2	
3		4
	5	

1 4	2 7	
3 5		4 1
	5 3	2

DIRECTIONS

For each problem, copy the grid here and fill it in.

You are given some of the answers to a problem. Arrange them so that they all fit into the grid. If you are given something like 3×4, find the product, 12, and fit 12 (not 3 and 4) into the grid.

There may be more than one way to arrange the answers, but you need find only one way.

If the answers you are given will not all fit into the grid, then tell why not.

1	2	
3		4
	5	

PROBLEMS

182. $35 \div 5 \times 8$; $14 + 7 \times 9$; $3^2 \times \sqrt{16}$; $150 \div 2$

183. For this problem, you are told where one of the answers must go.

$4 \times 5 + 21$; $3 \times 8 + 2 \times 6$; 4-D $= 2 \times 7^2 - 7$; $\sqrt{25} \times 7$

184. 47, 48, 17, 35

Reference

Math Mind Benders®— Warm Up & Warm Up–2

LESSON

Here is a sample problem. You will see that a short story is followed by clues that tell you where the answers go. No answer begins with 0.

You will not necessarily be able to fill in the answers in the same order as the clues are given.

SAMPLE PROBLEM

Ramona is 2 years older than Lance, who is 3 years older than Horace. Ramona's great-aunt Martha is a jet pilot.

ACROSS
1. Age of Pat, Ramona's sister
3. Test problems Ramona got wrong yesterday
4. Lance's age
5. 4 × half of 1-A

DOWN
1. Ramona's age
2. Horace's age
4. Age of Great-aunt Martha's father
5. Age of Spot, Ramona's cat

Only clues 4-A, 1-D, and 2-D are connected with the story. Notice that 1-D is a two-digit answer, and 4-A is a one-digit answer.

1-D is 2 more than 4-A (given in the story), so 1-D must be 10 or 11. If 1-D were 10, then 3-A would be 0, which is forbidden. So 1-D is 11, and 4-A is 9. Then 2-D is 6.

Reference

*Math
Mind
Benders®—
Warm Up
& Warm
Up–2*

Here is the sample problem again, along with what we have filled in so far.

SAMPLE PROBLEM

Ramona is 2 years older than Lance, who is 3 years older than Horace. Ramona's great-aunt Martha is a jet pilot.

ACROSS
1. Age of Pat, Ramona's sister
3. Test problems Ramona got wrong yesterday
4. Lance's age
5. 4 × half of 1-A

DOWN
1. Ramona's age
2. Horace's age
4. Age of Great-aunt Martha's father
5. Age of Spot, Ramona's cat

¹1	²6	
³1		⁴9
	⁵	

Now go to clue 5-A, which says to take 4 × half of 1-A. Half of 1-A is 8. Then 4 × 8 = 32, so 5-A is 32.

¹1	²6	
³1		⁴9
	⁵3	2

All squares are filled in now. We go back and read the clues we have ignored until now, in order to make sure there are no contradictions. These are clues 1-A, 3-A, 4-D, and 5-D. In each case, the answer is suitable.

Reference

*Math
Mind
Benders®—
Book B–1*

DIRECTIONS

In the clues, "A" means across, and "D" means down. For example, "4-D" would refer to clue number 4 DOWN.

Each square takes a single digit from 0 through 9. No answer begins with 0.

PROBLEM

185. Last week Yuan-Jai, Eleanor, and Uhle, three teenagers of different ages, went on a hay ride sponsored by their local Youth Club. Uhle's great-aunt Martha was one of the volunteers who had hot chocolate and sandwiches ready for everyone when the ride was over.

ACROSS
   1. Sandwiches Yuan-Jai ate
   2. 4-A × 3
   4. Yuan-Jai's age
   6. See 3-D
   7. Product of 5 more and 5 less than half the sum of 4-A, 3-D, and 8-D
   9. See 11-D
   10. 4 × 4-A

DOWN
   1. 4-A × 3-D × 8-D
   2. Times Uhle got pushed off the hay wagon
   3. Eleanor's age
   5. Age of Washington, Great-aunt Martha's husband
   8. Uhle's age
   11. See 9-A

1		2	3
4	5		6
7		8	
9		10	11

Reference

Math Mind Benders®— Book B–1

DIRECTIONS

In the clues, "A" means across, and "D" means down. For example, "4-D" would refer to clue number 4 DOWN.

Each square takes a single digit from 0 through 9. No answer begins with 0.

PROBLEM

186. Judy's uncle Norton is 4 times as old as Judy, who is 4 times as old as Selena. Judy's great-aunt Martha is a pilot for Star Transair, a private airline specializing in the transport of celebrities.

ACROSS
1. See 1-D
2. Half of 5-D
4. Age of Anna, Great-aunt Martha's grandmother
6. Judy's age
7. Square of sum of 8-D and 6-A
9. Trips Great-aunt Martha made for Star Transair last month
10. Uncle Norton's age

DOWN
1. 10-A + square of 5-D
2. Times Great-aunt Martha has made forced landings
3. Age of Paul, Great-aunt Martha's father
5. Age of Great-aunt Martha
8. Sum of digits of 6-A and 10-A
11. Age of Selena

1		2	3
4	5		6
7		8	
9		10	11

MISCELLANEOUS PROBLEMS

PROBLEM

187.   Of the students in the eleventh grade, 20 were taking both an American literature class and an advanced grammar class, 45 were taking an American literature class, and 50 were taking an advanced grammar class.

How many students

a. were taking American literature but not advanced grammar?

b. were taking advanced grammar but not American literature?

c. are mentioned in this problem?

The government closed down an army base and sold all government-issued furniture that had been in the houses on the base. What did the little kid expect to find in the bureau his parents bought at the sale?

CLOCK ARITHMETIC

LESSON

Suppose we had a clock that went only from 1 to 8 instead of from 1 to 12. We could do the same kind of arithmetic with it that we do for a 12-hour clock.

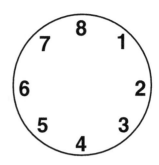

With a 12-hour clock, we count from 1 to 12 and then start over. With an 8-hour clock, we would count from 1 to 8 and then start over.

EXAMPLES

If it is 5 o'clock now, then 4 hours from now it will be 1 o'clock.

If it is 2 o'clock now, then 2 hours ago it was 8 o'clock, and 3 hours ago it was 7 o'clock.

DIRECTIONS

You are told what time it is now. You are asked to find a different time. Use an 8-hour clock.

EXAMPLE

Problem: 7 o'clock; 2 hours from now
Answer: 1 o'clock

PROBLEMS

188. 7 o'clock; 3 hours from now

189. 3 o'clock; 3 hours ago

190. 6 o'clock; 8 hours from now

191. 6 o'clock; 8 hours ago

192. 5 o'clock; 6 hours from now

193. 4 o'clock; 9 hours from now

194. 1 o'clock; 6 hours ago

195. 7 o'clock; 12 hours ago

DIRECTIONS

Now try analogous ideas on other clocks.

EXAMPLE

Problem: 6-hour clock; now 5 o'clock; 3 hours from now
Answer: 2 o'clock

PROBLEMS

196.   6-hour clock; now 5 o'clock; 7 hours from now

197.   7-hour clock; now 2 o'clock; 5 hours ago

198.   10-hour clock; now 8 o'clock; 7 hours from now

199.   4-hour clock; now 3 o'clock; 3 hours from now

200.   9-hour clock; now 2 o'clock; 24 hours ago

201.   5-hour clock; now 3 o'clock; 12 hours ago

202. MARIO'S METHOD FOR CLOCK ARITHMETIC

Mario says he has a fast way of doing clock arithmetic. He gave these examples:

"Suppose it's a 6-hour clock. If my answer is more than 6, I subtract 6. If it's going to be less than 1, I add 6. Say it's 4 o'clock and I want 5 hours from now. I take 4 + 5 and get 9. That's more than 6, so I subtract 6 and get 3, so the answer is 3 o'clock.

"Or say it's 1 o'clock and I want 3 hours ago. If I take 1 − 3, I'll get less than 1, so I add 6 first. I take 1 + 6 − 3 and get 4, so the answer is 4 o'clock."

Julia asked what happens if his answer is still more than 6 for a 6-hour clock. He said he keeps subtracting 6's until the answer is between 1 and 6. Julia used Mario's method to find the time 8 hours after 5 o'clock. She took 8 + 5 − 6 − 6 and got 1 o'clock, and that answer is correct.

Loretta asked Mario what he does for a 6-hour clock if the problem says to find the time 16 hours ago if it's 2 o'clock now. He said he keeps adding 6's to the 2 until he gets a number more than 16, and then he subtracts.

a. Do you think Mario's method will <u>always</u> work for a 6-hour clock? If so, how come? If not, give a counterexample.

b. 1) What would Mario's method be for a 9-hour clock?

    2) Do you think his method will work for a 9-hour clock? If so, how come? If not, give a counterexample.

c. Do you think Mario's method will work for other clocks? If so, how come? If not, give a counterexample.

203. CHOON-WEI'S METHOD FOR CLOCK ARITHMETIC

Choon-Wei said she has a fast method for doing clock arithmetic, too.

For a 6-hour clock, she does the same as Mario if the hours to be added or subtracted are less than 6. But if those hours are more than 6, she subtracts 6's right away.

Choon-Wei gave these examples:

"Say it's 3 o'clock now and I want to know the time 14 hours from now. I take 14 – 6 – 6 and get 2, and then I add that to 3 and get 5, so it will be 5 o'clock then.

"Or say it's 3 o'clock now and I want the time 14 hours ago. I take 14 – 6 – 6 and get 2, and I subtract that from 3 and get 1, so it was 1 o'clock then."

Larry said her method wouldn't work for a problem like 14 hours ago if it's 1 o'clock now, because 14 – 6 – 6 is 2, and 1 – 2 is less than 1. Choon-Wei said he was wrong, because his example reduced the problem to finding the time 2 hours ago if it's 1 o'clock now, and she already said that she uses Mario's method for that kind of problem.

a. Do you think Choon-Wei's method will <u>always</u> work for a 6-hour clock? If so, how come? If not, give a counterexample.

b. Suppose Choon-Wei uses analogous reasoning for a 7-hour clock. How would she find the time 15 hours from now if it is now 2 o'clock?

c. Do you think Choon-Wei's method will work for other clocks? If so, how come? If not, give a counterexample.

LESSON

In the United States, the official time period known as a "day" starts at 12 midnight, written as either

12 midnight   or   12 A.M.

The A.M. hours continue from then until 12 noon, which is written as

12 noon   or   12 P.M.

The P.M. hours last from then until midnight.

To do clock arithmetic for a real-life 12-hour clock, we need to know whether the answer is A.M. or P.M. This is easy to do if we use a 24-hour clock for our figuring. On a 24-hour clock, the A.M. hours start at 24 and go through 11. The P.M. hours start at 12 and go through 23.

When given a problem, we will first convert the starting time to the time on a 24-hour clock. Then we will do the problem. After we have decided whether the hour is A.M. or P.M., we will convert the answer to 12-hour clock time.

EXAMPLE 1

Problem: It is 3 A.M. now. What time will it be 10 hours from now?

Solution: 3 A.M. = 3 on a 24-hour clock. 3 + 10 = 13, which is a P.M. hour. 13 on this clock is 1 on a 12-hour clock, so it will be 1 P.M.

EXAMPLE 2

Problem: It is 3 A.M. now. What time was it 10 hours ago?

Solution: 3 A.M. = 3 on a 24-hour clock. 3 – 10 is negative, so add 24 to 3. Then 27 – 10 = 17, which is a P.M. hour. 17 – 12 = 5 on a 12-hour clock, so the answer is 5 P.M.

DIRECTIONS FOR PROBLEMS 204–8

You are given the time now on a 12-hour clock and are asked to find the time some hours before or after that.

Include A.M. or P.M. in your answer.

PROBLEMS 204–8

204. Now 2 P.M.; 4 hours ago

205. Now 4 A.M.; 9 hours from now

206. Now 4 A.M.; 9 hours ago

207. Now 6 P.M.; 8 hours from now

208. Now 5 P.M.; 8 hours ago

PROBLEM

209. Given that we'll use a 24-hour clock so that we'll know whether our answer is A.M. or P.M., why bother to convert the starting time to 24-hour clock time?

That is, why not leave the starting time alone and just add to it or subtract from it the hours in the problem, and then convert the answer if it needs converting?

For example, if it's 3 P.M. now, then 7 hours from now it will be 3 + 7 = 10 P.M. We don't have to bother converting 3 to 15, getting 15 + 7 = 22, and then converting 22 to 10.

DIRECTIONS

The U.S. Armed Forces and many scientific laboratories use a 24-hour clock. This clock is numbered from 100 through 2400 instead of from 1 through 24. At 6 P.M. the time is said to be 1800. On this clock, the time 3 hours after 1800 is 2100.

You are given the time on such a 24-hour clock. You are asked to find the time some hours earlier or later.

Keep in mind that the clock numbers are 100 times the actual numbers, so you will have to adjust one or the other in order to find an answer.

EXAMPLE

Problem: Now 0300; 7 hours ago

Solution 1: Convert 7 hours to 700 clock hours. 300 – 700 is less than 100, so add 2400 to 300. Then the time asked for is 2700 – 700 = 2000.

Solution 2: Convert 0300 to 3. 3 – 7 is less than 1, so add 24 to 3. Then 27 – 7 = 20. Convert 20 to clock hours, 2000, to get the time asked for.

PROBLEMS

210.   Now 0300; 14 hours from now

211.   Now 0300; 14 hours ago

212.   Now 1600; 20 hours from now

213.   Now 0600; 10 hours ago

214.   Now 1100; 14 hours from now

215.   Now 1850; 7 hours from now

CONGRUENCES (MODULAR ARITHMETIC)

LESSON

The statement

$$15 \equiv 3 \text{ (mod 12)}$$

is supposed to be read as "15 is congruent to 3 modulus [or modulo] 12," but most people shorten it to "15 is congruent to 3 mod 12." The statement is called a **congruence**.

We can use such a statement for clock arithmetic. The congruence above says that we have a 12-hour clock (mod 12) and that we end up with 3 when we take 15 and subtract 12 from it.

A congruence can also be written when we have to subtract more than one 12, or when we have to add 12's, as shown in these statements:

$$39 \equiv 3 \text{ (mod 12)}$$

$$10 + 15 \equiv 1 \text{ (mod 12)}$$

$$7 - 8 \equiv 7 - 8 + 12 \text{ (mod 12)} \equiv 11 \text{ (mod 12)}$$

The clock doesn't have to be a 12-hour clock.

$$16 \equiv 2 \text{ (mod 7)}$$

uses a 7-hour clock, and

$$10 \equiv 1 \text{ (mod 3)}$$

uses a 3-hour clock.

We could also write statements like these two:

$$2 - 28 + 48 = 22 \equiv 10 \text{ (mod 12)}$$

$$6 + 28 = 34 \equiv 4 \text{ (mod 6)}$$

We would read this last statement as, "6 + 28 = 34, which is congruent to 4 mod 6."

DIRECTIONS

You are told the time now and asked to find the time some hours earlier or later on a given clock. Use a congruence to show the answer.

EXAMPLE

Problem: Now 7 o'clock; 25 hours from now; 9-hour clock

Answer: $7 + 25 = 32 \equiv 5 \pmod 9$

PROBLEMS

216.   Now 7 o'clock; 30 hours from now; 9-hour clock

217.   Now 5 o'clock; 8 hours from now; 6-hour clock

218.   Now 5 o'clock; 8 hours ago; 6-hour clock

219.   Now 3 o'clock; 11 hours ago; 5-hour clock

220.   Now 8 o'clock; 24 hours from now; 10-hour clock

221.   Now 3 o'clock; 10 hours from now; 2-hour clock

222.   Now 6 o'clock; 15 hours ago; 16-hour clock

LESSON

We have used clock arithmetic on different clocks and found the arithmetic analogous for all clocks.

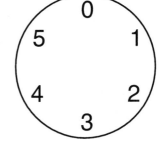

Now think about a 6-hour clock whose "6" has been replaced with "0." The clock will still have 6 numbers, but they will go from 0 through 5 instead of from 1 through 6.

Suppose it is now 1 o'clock. Then 5 hours from now it would be 1 + 5 = 6 o'clock, except that our clock's 6 is now a 0, so it will be 0 o'clock. We can write the statement

$$1 + 5 = 6 \equiv 0 \pmod 6$$

to show this.

We will work problems in exactly the same way we worked problems for a 6-hour clock whose numbers were 1 through 6. No change will show up unless we get a final answer of 6, in which case our answer will be 0 instead.

EXAMPLES

Problem: Find the time 3 hours after 1 o'clock.
Answer: $1 + 3 \equiv 4 \pmod 6$

Problem: Find the time 3 hours after 5 o'clock.
Answer: $5 + 3 = 8 \equiv 2 \pmod 6$

Problem: Find the time 14 hours after 4 o'clock.
Answer: $4 + 14 = 18 \equiv 0 \pmod 6$

Problem: Find the time 7 hours before 3 o'clock.
Answer 1: $3 - 7 \equiv 3 - 7 + 6 \pmod 6 = 2 \pmod 6$
Answer 2: $3 - 7 + 6 = 2 \equiv 2 \pmod 6$
Answer 3: $3 - 7 \equiv 2 \pmod 6$

DIRECTIONS

You have a 6-hour clock whose numbers run from 0 through 5. You are asked to find the time some number of hours before or after a given starting time. Use a congruence to express your answer.

EXAMPLE

Problem: Now 4 o'clock; 7 hours later

Answer: $4 + 7 = 11 \equiv 5$ (mod 6)

PROBLEMS

223.   Now 1 o'clock; 7 hours later

224.   Now 3 o'clock; 5 hours earlier

225.   Now 5 o'clock; 13 hours later

226.   Now 0 o'clock; 11 hours later

227.   Now 2 o'clock; 10 hours earlier

228.   Now 4 o'clock; 45 hours from now

229.   Now 4 o'clock; 45 hours ago

DIRECTIONS

Express each number as a congruence having a modulus of 6. Your final result must be in the range of 0 through 5.

EXAMPLE

Problem: $35 + (16 - 3)$

Answer: $35 + (16 - 3) = 35 + 13 = 48 \equiv 0 \pmod 6$

PROBLEMS

230. $39 - (25 + 4)$

231. $4 \times 8 - 20$

232. $3^2 + 16$

233. 3 less than the product of 2 and 8

DIRECTIONS

Express each number as a congruence using the modulus specified. Your final result must be a number in the range of 0 to (not including) the modulus.

PROBLEMS

234. $8 + 11$; mod 5

235. $4 + 29 - 17$; mod 7

236. $3 \times 6 + 10 - 4$; mod 10

237. $29 - 22 - 10$; mod 5

238. $12 + 2 - 19$; mod 4

LESSON

You have learned to write congruences of the form

$$a \equiv b \ (\text{mod } c),$$

where a, b, and c are integers.

EXAMPLE

Given the general statement

$$a \equiv b \ (\text{mod } c),$$

then for

$$11 \equiv 5 \ (\text{mod } 6),$$

$a = 11$, $b = 5$, and $c = 6$.

The quick way to tell whether or not two numbers are congruent (for a given modulus) is to use the definition of congruence:

DEFINITION OF CONGRUENCE

When a, b, and c are integers, $c > 0$, the statement

$$a \equiv b \ (\text{mod } c)$$

means the same as the statement

$$\frac{a - b}{c} \text{ is an integer.}$$

If $a - b < 0$, you may use $b - a$.

Here are some examples of how to use the definition. Keep referring to the definition as you read each example.

EXAMPLE 1

(Notice that "$\overset{?}{\equiv}$" is used instead of "$\equiv$" in the problem. This is a short way of asking if the statement is true.)

Problem: $45 \overset{?}{\equiv} 20 \ (\text{mod } 8)$

Solution: $(45 - 20)/8 = 25/8$. Since $25/8$ is not integral, 45 and 20 are not congruent. Notice that we did not have to know the answer to $25/8$. It was enough to know that $25/8$ is not a whole number.

Answer: $45 \not\equiv 20 \ (\text{mod } 8)$

EXAMPLE 2

Problem: Using modulus 6, is 5 congruent to 15?

Solution: The problem is: $5 \overset{?}{\equiv} 15 \ (\text{mod } 6)$. We see that $5 - 15$ is less than 0, so we use $15 - 5$. We get $(15 - 5)/6 = 10/6$, which is not a whole number.

Answer: $5 \not\equiv 15 \ (\text{mod } 6)$

DIRECTIONS

You are given two numbers and a modulus.

Use the definition of congruence to decide whether or not the numbers are congruent for that modulus.

Here is the definition again:

DEFINITION OF CONGRUENCE

When a, b, and c are integers, $c > 0$, the statement

$$a \equiv b \,(\text{mod } c)$$

means the same as the statement

$$\frac{a-b}{c} \text{ is an integer.}$$

If $a - b < 0$, you may use $b - a$.

Show your work. Show your final answer as a congruence or a noncongruence.

EXAMPLES

Problem: 5, 25, mod 4

Answer: $(25 - 5)/4 = 20/4 = 5$, so $5 \equiv 25 \,(\text{mod } 4)$.

Problem: 24, 4, mod 6

Answer: $(24 - 4)/6 = 20/6$. $20/6$ is not a whole number, so $24 \not\equiv 4 \,(\text{mod } 6)$.

Problem: $26 - 4 \times 5$, 12, mod 3

Answer: (first step): $26 - 4 \times 5 = 26 - 20 = 6$.

(second step): $(12 - 6)/3 = 6/3 = 2$. (This shows that $\dfrac{12 - (26 - 4 \times 5)}{3}$ is a whole number.) So $26 - 4 \times 5 \equiv 12 \,(\text{mod } 3)$.

PROBLEMS

239.   18, 3, mod 5

240. 7, 13, mod 3

241. 25 − 20, 16, mod 12

242. 7×8, 4×8, mod 6

243. 17 − 12 + 20, 11, mod 7

244. 23 + 12, $3 \times 5 + 3^2$, mod 11

245. 14 + 16/4, 4×2, mod 10

246. $(4 \times 6 + 3 \times 12)/4$, $15 \times 3 - 4 \times 10$, mod 8

247. Suppose a and b have a common factor. Then will $a \equiv b \pmod{c}$ always be a true statement if c

    a. also has this factor? If so, tell why. If not, give a counterexample.

    b. does not have this factor? If so, tell why. If not, give a counterexample.

248. Given $a \equiv b \pmod{c}$,

    a. if b is a factor of a, does b also have to be a factor of c? If so, tell why. If not, give a counterexample.

    b. if a and b are prime numbers, does c also have to be a prime number? If so, tell why. If not, give a counterexample.

    c. if a and b are not prime numbers, can c be a prime number? If not, tell why. If so, give an example.

All letters used as placeholders represent integers.

Definition: If $a \equiv b$ (mod c), then $\dfrac{a-b}{c}$ is an integer.

249. Prove that for a given modulus,

　　a. any integer is congruent to itself.

　　b. the number used as the modulus is congruent to 0.

　　c. any integral multiple of the number used as the modulus is congruent to 0.

　　The problem can also be stated like this:
　　Prove that for any integers n, a and c, where $c > 0$,

　　a. $a \equiv a$ (mod c)

　　b. $c \equiv 0$ (mod c)

　　c. n times $c \equiv 0$ (mod c)

All letters used as placeholders represent integers.

Definition: If $a \equiv b \pmod{c}$, then $\dfrac{a-b}{c}$ is an integer.

Free information: If $\dfrac{r-s}{t}$ is an integer, then so is $\dfrac{s-r}{t}$.

These are problems proved earlier:

64. a. $(r-s)-t = r-(s+t)$. Or, $r-s-t = r-(s+t)$.
    b. $r-(s-t) = (r-s)+t$. Or, $r-(s-t) = r-s+t$.
    c. $(r-s)+t = (r+t)-s$. Or, $r-s+t = r+t-s$.
    d. $(r-s)-t = (r-t)-s$. Or, $r-s-t = r-t-s$.

249. a. $a \equiv a \pmod{c}$
     b. $c \equiv 0 \pmod{c}$
     c. n times $c \equiv 0 \pmod{c}$

250. Show that if one number is congruent to another, then the second is congruent to the first.

   Here is another way to state the problem: Tell why

$$\text{if } a \equiv b \pmod{c}, \text{ then } b \equiv a \pmod{c}.$$

251. You are given a modulus and three numbers. Show why

   a. if the first number is congruent to the second, and the second is congruent to the third, then the first is congruent to the third.

   b. if the first and third numbers are both congruent to the second, then the first is congruent to the third.

   Here is another way to state the problem: Show why

   a. if $a \equiv b \pmod{c}$
      and if $b \equiv d \pmod{c}$,
      then $a \equiv d \pmod{c}$.

   b. if $a \equiv b \pmod{c}$
      and if $d \equiv b \pmod{c}$,
      then $a \equiv d \pmod{c}$.

All letters used as placeholders represent integers.

Definition: If $a \equiv b$ (mod c), then $\dfrac{a-b}{c}$ is an integer.

These are problems proved earlier:

64. a. $(r-s)-t = r-(s+t)$. Or, $r-s-t = r-(s+t)$.

 b. $r-(s-t) = (r-s)+t$. Or, $r-(s-t) = r-s+t$.

 c. $(r-s)+t = (r+t)-s$. Or, $r-s+t = r+t-s$.

 d. $(r-s)-t = (r-t)-s$. Or, $r-s-t = r-t-s$.

250. If $a \equiv b$ (mod c), then $b \equiv a$ (mod c).

252. Prove that if two numbers are congruent, then

 a. their doubles are congruent.

 b. if both numbers are multiplied by the same third number, the results will be congruent.

253. You may use any of the references given at the top of this page, but you may **not** use any knowledge you have of how to work with negative numbers.

Suppose you are asked to determine whether or not the numbers

$$3 - 22$$

and

$$7$$

are congruent in modulus 4.

How would you solve this problem?

All letters used as placeholders represent integers.

Definition: If $a \equiv b \pmod{c}$, then $\dfrac{a-b}{c}$ is an integer.

These are problems proved earlier:

64.   a. $(r-s)-t = r-(s+t)$. Or, $r-s-t = r-(s+t)$.

      b. $r-(s-t) = (r-s)+t$. Or, $r-(s-t) = r-s+t$.

      c. $(r-s)+t = (r+t)-s$. Or, $r-s+t = r+t-s$.

      d. $(r-s)-t = (r-t)-s$. Or, $r-s-t = r-t-s$.

250. If $a \equiv b \pmod{c}$, then $b \equiv a \pmod{c}$.

---

254. You are given a modulus and two pairs of numbers, say pair #1 and pair #2.

Pair #1 are congruent, and pair #2 are congruent.

Tell why these statements are true:

a. If you add pair #2 to pair #1 (first number to first number, second to second), then the sums are congruent.

b. If you subtract pair #2 from pair #1 (first number from first number, second from second), then the differences are congruent.

The problem can be stated like this: Tell why,

if $a \equiv b \pmod{c}$

and if $e \equiv f \pmod{c}$,

a. then $a + e \equiv b + f \pmod{c}$

b. and then $a - e \equiv b - f \pmod{c}$.

All letters used as placeholders represent integers.

Definition: If $a \equiv b$ (mod c), then $\dfrac{a-b}{c}$ is an integer.

These are problems proved earlier:

249. c. n times $c \equiv 0$ (mod c)

250. If $a \equiv b$ (mod c), then $b \equiv a$ (mod c).

251. a. If $a \equiv b$ (mod c) and if $b \equiv d$ (mod c), then $a \equiv d$ (mod c).

254. If $a \equiv b$ (mod c) and if $e \equiv f$ (mod c), then

    a. $a + e \equiv b + f$ (mod c)

    b. $a - e \equiv b - f$ (mod c).

255. You are given $a \equiv b$ (mod c).

Explain why you can add or subtract any multiple of c to either a or b and still have a congruence.

Further, explain why you can add or subtract one multiple of c to a, and a different multiple of c to b, and still have a congruence.

Here is the problem expressed in symbols:
Given $a \equiv b$ (mod c) and the integers $m > 0$, $n > 0$, explain why

a. $a + nc \equiv b$ (mod c)

b. $a - nc \equiv b$ (mod c)

c. $a \equiv b + mc$ (mod c)

d. $a \equiv b - mc$ (mod c)

e. $a + nc \equiv b + mc$ (mod c)

f. $a - nc \equiv b + mc$ (mod c)

g. $a + nc \equiv b - mc$ (mod c)

h. $a - nc \equiv b - mc$ (mod c)

Hint: You don't really need to do eight proofs for this problem. Figure out how to do the first one by using problems already proved, and then use analogous reasoning on the others.

All letters used as placeholders represent integers.

Definition: If $a \equiv b \pmod{c}$, then $\dfrac{a - b}{c}$ is an integer.

These are problems proved earlier:

249. a. $a \equiv a \pmod{c}$

250. If $a \equiv b \pmod{c}$, then $b \equiv a \pmod{c}$.

251. a. If $a \equiv b \pmod{c}$ and if $b \equiv d \pmod{c}$, then $a \equiv d \pmod{c}$.

254. If $a \equiv b \pmod{c}$ and if $e \equiv f \pmod{c}$, then

a. $a + e \equiv b + f \pmod{c}$

b. $a - e \equiv b - f \pmod{c}$.

256. You are given $a \equiv b \pmod{c}$ and an integer $n \geq 0$.

Show that if n is added to or subtracted from both a and b, or if both a and b are added to or subtracted from n, the result is still a congruence.

Here is another way to state the problem:
Given an integer $n \geq 0$, and given $a \equiv b \pmod{c}$, prove

a. $a + n \equiv b + n \pmod{c}$

b. $a - n \equiv b - n \pmod{c}$

c. $n + a \equiv n + b \pmod{c}$

d. $n - a \equiv n - b \pmod{c}$

Hint: Instead of doing four proofs, find a way to do part **a** by using problems already proved, and then apply analogous reasoning to the other parts.

All letters used as placeholders represent integers.

Definition: If $a \equiv b$ (mod c), then $\frac{a-b}{c}$ is an integer.

These are problems proved earlier:

249.   a. $a \equiv a$ (mod c)

b. $c \equiv 0$ (mod c)

c. n times $c \equiv 0$ (mod c)

250.   If $a \equiv b$ (mod c), then $b \equiv a$ (mod c).

251.   a. If $a \equiv b$ (mod c) and if $b \equiv d$ (mod c), then $a \equiv d$ (mod c).

b. If $a \equiv b$ (mod c) and if $d \equiv b$ (mod c), then $a \equiv d$ (mod c).

254.   If $a \equiv b$ (mod c) and if $e \equiv f$ (mod c), then

a. $a + e \equiv b + f$ (mod c)

b. $a - e \equiv b - f$ (mod c).

257.   Suppose $a \equiv b$ (mod c), where a and b have a common factor f.

a. If f is a prime number, must f also be a factor of c? If so, tell why. If not, give a counterexample.

b. If f is not a prime number, must f be a factor of c? If so, tell why. If not, give a counterexample.

258.   Suppose $a \equiv b$ (mod c), where a and c have a common factor f.

a. Must f also be a factor of b? If so, tell why. If not, give a counterexample.

b. Can b be a multiple of a prime number? If so, give an example. If not, tell why.

All letters used as placeholders represent integers.

Definition: If $a \equiv b \pmod{c}$, then $\frac{a-b}{c}$ is an integer.

These are problems proved earlier:

64.　a.　$(r-s) - t = r - (s+t)$. Or, $r - s - t = r - (s+t)$.

　　　b.　$r - (s-t) = (r-s) + t$. Or, $r - (s-t) = r - s + t$.

　　　c.　$(r-s) + t = (r+t) - s$. Or, $r - s + t = r + t - s$.

　　　d.　$(r-s) - t = (r-t) - s$. Or, $r - s - t = r - t - s$.

249.　a.　$a \equiv a \pmod{c}$

　　　c.　n times $c \equiv 0 \pmod{c}$

250.　If $a \equiv b \pmod{c}$, then $b \equiv a \pmod{c}$.

251.　a.　If $a \equiv b \pmod{c}$ and if $b \equiv d \pmod{c}$, then $a \equiv d \pmod{c}$.

　　　b.　If $a \equiv b \pmod{c}$ and if $d \equiv b \pmod{c}$, then $a \equiv d \pmod{c}$.

252.　If $a \equiv b \pmod{c}$, then n times $a \equiv n$ times $b \pmod{c}$.

254.　If $a \equiv b \pmod{c}$ and if $e \equiv f \pmod{c}$, then

　　　a.　$a + e \equiv b + f \pmod{c}$

　　　b.　$a - e \equiv b - f \pmod{c}$.

255.　[Put $nc = n$ times c, $mc = m$ times c.] If $a \equiv b \pmod{c}$, then

　　　$a \pm nc \equiv b \pmod{c}$, and $a \equiv b \pm mc \pmod{c}$, and

　　　$a + nc \equiv b \pm mc \pmod{c}$, and $a - nc \equiv b \pm mc \pmod{c}$.

256.　If $a \equiv b \pmod{c}$, then $a \pm n \equiv b \pm n \pmod{c}$, and then $n \pm a \equiv n \pm b \pmod{c}$.

259.　What else can you discover about congruences?

Hint: There are a great many things you could find out about congruences. For example:

A. If $a \equiv b \pmod{c}$,

　　a.　and if f divides $a - b$, must f divide c?

　　b.　and if f divides both a and b, then is $\frac{a}{f} \equiv \frac{b}{f} \pmod{c}$?

[Problem continued on next page.]

A. (continued) If $a \equiv b$ (mod c),

     c. is $a^2 \equiv b^2$ (mod c)?

     d. is $a^n \equiv b^n$ (mod c)?

     e. is $a^2 \equiv b^2$ (mod c^2)?

B. If $a \equiv b$ (mod c) and $d \equiv e$ (mod c),

     a. is $a - e \equiv b - d$ (mod c)?

     b. is a times $d \equiv b$ times e (mod c)?

     c. is a times $e \equiv b$ times d (mod c)?

     d. and if d divides a, and e divides b, is $\dfrac{a}{d} \equiv \dfrac{b}{e}$ (mod c)?

C. If $a \equiv b$ (mod c) and $d \equiv e$ (mod f),

     a. is $a + d \equiv b + e$ (mod $c + f$)?

     b. is a times $d \equiv b$ times e (mod c times f)?

There are many other questions that could be asked about congruences. What questions can you think of?

OTHER BASES

LESSON, PART I

Think about the way we write numbers. We start with only ten digits:

0 1 2 3 4 5 6 7 8 9

The first digit, 0, is for zero. After that, they mean 0 + 1, 0 + 2, 0 + 3, and so on, up through 0 + 9.

We don't invent new digits when we want to write a number past 9. Instead, we use what we already have, but we write them side by side:

10 11 12 13 14 15 16 17 18 19

Notice that this row of numbers is exactly like the top row, except that each number in this row starts with 1. This 1 means that we've used all ten of our digits once before, and we've started over again.

The first symbol here, 10, is for ten because we had ten digits. After that, they mean 10 + 1, 10 + 2, 10 + 3, and so on, up through 10 + 9.

After we've written 19, we've used our ten digits twice apiece, so each number in the next row starts with 2:

20 21 22 23 24 25 26 27 28 29

The first symbol here, 20, is for two tens, 2×10. After that, they mean $(2 \times 10) + 1$, $(2 \times 10) + 2$, $(2 \times 10) + 3$, and so on, up through $(2 \times 10) + 9$.

We keep going the same way up through the 90s:

90 91 92 93 94 95 96 97 98 99

This time the first symbol, 90, is for nine tens, 9×10. The others mean $(9 \times 10) + 1$, $(9 \times 10) + 2$, $(9 \times 10) + 3$, and so on, up through $(9 \times 10) + 9$.

When we reached 90, we had used all ten of our digits 9 times before. Now that we've written 99, we've used all ten digits 10 times, and we have no digits left to write a higher number.

We had an analogous problem after we wrote the number 9. We had used all ten digits once and had to think of a way to write ten, the next number after nine.

We solved that problem by starting at 0 again but writing 1 to the left of 0 to show that the ten digits had all been used one time before.

We will solve this problem in an analogous way. We'll start at 0 again but write 10 to the left of it to show that we've used all ten digits ten times: $100 = 10 \times 10$.

To be more exact, 100 really means

$$1 \times (10 \times 10) \quad + \quad 0 \times 10 \quad + \quad 0 \times 1.$$

Here are some other examples:

$$205 = 2 \times (10 \times 10) \quad + \quad 0 \times 10 \quad + \quad 5 \times 1$$

$$359 = 3 \times (10 \times 10) \quad + \quad 5 \times 10 \quad + \quad 9 \times 1$$

Notice that we write numbers in a special way:

The last digit (on the right) tells how many 1s there are.

$$7 = 7 \times 1$$

The digit to the left of it tells how many 10s there are.

$$37 = 3 \times 10 \quad + \quad 7 \times 1$$

The digit to the left of that one tells how many (10×10)'s there are.

$$637 = 6 \times (10 \times 10) \quad + \quad 3 \times 10 \quad + \quad 7 \times 1$$

LESSON, PART II

Because we use ten different digits to write numbers, we say that we use a **base** of ten to write them, or that we write them in **base ten**.

Look at 637 again. Each place held by a digit means something different. Going from right to left, the first digit is in the 1s place, the second digit is in the 10s place, and the third digit is in the (10×10)'s place.

For a four-digit number, the fourth digit would be in the $(10 \times 10 \times 10)$'s place. And so on.

Now suppose we didn't have ten different digits. Suppose there were only five different digits—0, 1, 2, 3, and 4. Then we would write the numbers in base five.

34 in base five = (in base ten) $3 \times 5 + 4$ = (in base ten) $15 + 4 = 19$.

Notice that we don't write "34 = 19," because that wouldn't make sense. Neither can we write "base 5" (because there is no "5" in base five) or "base 10" (because "10" means different things in different bases).

We could show the base by subscripts:

$$34_{five} = (3 \times 5 + 4)_{ten} = (15 + 4)_{ten} = 19_{ten}.$$

Or we could use columns:

Base five	Base ten
34	$3 \times 5 + 4 = 15 + 4 = 19$
201	$2 \times (5 \times 5) + 0 \times 5 + 1 \times 1 = 50 + 0 + 1 = 51$
37	Cannot convert. There is no "7" in base five.

Other bases work analogously to bases ten and five. When a number base is higher than ten, letters are used for the extra digits needed.

Base eight (also called an octal base):

1 2 3 4 5 6 7 10 11 12 13 14 15 16 17 20

Base ten (also called a decimal base):

1 2 3 4 5 6 7 8 9 10 11 12 13 14 15 16

Base twelve (also called a duodecimal base):

1 2 3 4 5 6 7 8 9 A B 10 11 12 13 14

Base sixteen (also called a hexadecimal base):

1 2 3 4 5 6 7 8 9 A B C D E F 10

DIRECTIONS

Convert each number to a base ten number.

PROBLEMS

260. 44_{five}

261. 36_{seven}

262. 28_{nine}

263. 145_{six}

264. 247_{eight}

265. 49_{twelve}

266. $3C_{sixteen}$

267. $2A1_{eleven}$

268. $A00_{sixteen}$

269. 10110011_{two}

LESSON

Think about how we add numbers in base ten. For example, to do this problem

$$\begin{array}{r} 247 \\ +56 \\ \hline \end{array}$$

we start by adding 7 and 6. We get 13, which can't all go in the 1s column, so we enter 3 in the 1s column and carry the other 10 to the 10s column.

$$\begin{array}{r} 1 \\ 247 \\ +56 \\ \hline 3 \end{array}$$

That's 1 ten we've carried there, so that column now has $(1 + 4 + 5)$ tens = 10 tens. We can't put 10 in one column, so we enter 0 there and carry the other 10 to the next column.

$$\begin{array}{r} 11 \\ 247 \\ +56 \\ \hline 03 \end{array}$$

That's 1 ten × ten we've carried there, so that column now has $(1 + 2)$ ten × tens = 3 ten × tens.

$$\begin{array}{r} 11 \\ 247 \\ +56 \\ \hline 303 \end{array}$$

Now that we've seen how base ten addition works, we can apply analogous reasoning to addition in other bases.

EXAMPLE

Problem: These are base eight digits. 166 + 75 = ?

Solution: $6 + 5 = 11_{ten} = 13_{eight}$. Enter 3 and carry 1. Then $1 + 6 + 7 = 14_{ten} = 16_{eight}$. Enter 6 and carry 1. Then $1 + 1 = 2$, so in base eight, $166 + 75 = 263$.

We check our base eight work by converting to base ten. $166_{eight} + 75_{eight} = 118_{ten} + 61_{ten} = 179_{ten}$. The answer of $263_{eight} = 179_{ten}$, so the answer checks out in base ten.

Answer: In base eight, 166 + 75 = 263.

DIRECTIONS

For each problem, assume the numbers are written in each of bases eight and eleven.

Check your work by converting to base ten.

Remember that the digits from zero through eleven in base eleven are

0, 1, 2, 3, 4, 5, 6, 7, 8, 9, A, 10.

EXAMPLE

Problem: 773 + 77

Discussion: The given numbers are <u>not</u> written in base ten. There are two separate problems here—one in base eight, and one in base eleven. For each one, we will add as indicated and then check the addition by converting to base ten.

Answer 1: base eight: 773 + 77 = 1072

base ten: 507 + 63 = 570; $1072_{eight} = 570_{ten}$

Answer 2: base eleven: 773 + 77 = 83A

base ten: 927 + 84 = 1011; $83A_{eleven} = 1011_{ten}$

PROBLEMS

270. 326 + 6

271. 134 + 56

272.   175 + 67

273.   475 + 65

274.   364 + 427

275.   777 + 777

276.   1000 + 500

277.   6354 + 4756

278. On the preceding page, 1000 + 500 was one of the problems.

We added in base eight and got an answer of 1500. So far, so good. That was nice and easy.

The first part of the conversion to base ten was easy, too. $1000_{eight} = 1 \times (8 \times 8 \times 8)_{ten} = 512_{ten}$.

Now how come when we converted the second number, 500, which is obviously 1/2 of 1000, we didn't get half of 512 (which is 256) but got 320 instead?

279. People who work with computers sometimes have to use the hexadecimal base.

Convert each base sixteen number to base ten.

a. 27

b. 2A

c. A9

d. AB

e. 2AB

f. FFF

LESSON

Going from right to left, the place values of a base five number are (in base ten):

1	$125 \ (= 5 \times 5 \times 5)$
5	$625 \ (= 5 \times 5 \times 5 \times 5)$
$25 \ (= 5 \times 5)$	and so on.

You know how to convert numbers from base five to base ten. Now suppose you have a base ten number that you want to write in base five. Here are the steps:

1) Ask: What is the highest place value of five that goes into the base ten number?
2) Ask: How many whole times will that value go into the number?
3) The answer to (2) will be the first digit of the base five number.
4) Multiply (1) by (2) and subtract the answer from the base ten number.
5) Repeat steps (1) through (4) until your base ten number is less than 5. This final number is the last digit of your base five number.

EXAMPLE

Problem: Convert 366_{ten} to base five.

Solution: 1)   625 is too large, so the highest place value is 125.
            2)   125 goes into 366 twice.
            3)   The first digit of the base five number is 2.
            4) $2 \times 125 = 250; \ 366 - 250 = 116$.

Return to step (1):

1)   25 is the highest place value of five that will go into 116.
2)   25 goes into 116 four times.
3)   The second digit of the base five number is 4. The base five number is 24 so far.
4) $4 \times 25 = 100; \ 116 - 100 = 16$.

Return to step (1) again:

1)   The highest place value is now 5.
2)   5 goes into 16 three times.
3)   The next digit of the base five number is 3, so the base five number is 243 so far.
4) $3 \times 5 = 15; \ 16 - 15 = 1$.
5)   1 is the last digit, so the base five number is 2431.

Answer: $366_{ten} = 2431_{five}$

DIRECTIONS

Each number is written in base ten. Convert it to base five.

PROBLEMS

280. 65

281. 119

282. 326

283. 1414

DIRECTIONS

Each number is written in base ten. Convert it to the base indicated.

Use reasoning analogous to the reasoning used for converting base ten numbers to base five numbers.

PROBLEMS

284. 45; six

285. 79; eight

286. 77; two

287. 539; nine

288. 3019; twelve

289. 6702; sixteen

DIRECTIONS

Convert each number to a base ten number and then to the base indicated.

EXAMPLE

Problem: 123_{five}; eight

Solution: 123_{five} = (in base ten) $1 \times (5 \times 5) + 2 \times 5 + 3 \times 1 = 25 + 10 + 3 = 38 = 4 \times 8 + 6 = 46_{eight}$

Answer: $123_{five} = 38_{ten} = 46_{eight}$

PROBLEMS

290. 33_{four}; five

291. 221_{three}; six

292. 244_{five}; eight

293. 2222_{four}; sixteen

294. $2222_{sixteen}$; four

295. $1324_{sixteen}$; twelve

296. 1001010_{two}; four

LESSON

Let's take a look at base ten subtraction:

```
    2  5  3
 -     6  7
 _____
```

We can't subtract 7 from 3, so we take a 10 from the tens column, and we make the problem (240 + 13) − (60 + 7).

```
       4  13
    2  5̶  3̶
 -     6  7
 _____
```

We enter our answer of 6 (for 13 − 7). In the tens column, we can't subtract 60 from 40, so we take a 100 from the ten × tens column and make the problem (100 + 140 + 13) − (60 + 7).

```
    1  14 13
    2̶  5̶  3̶
 -     6  7
 _____
             6
```

Let's be honest. We don't really think of subtracting 60 from 40 and then taking a 100 from the next column. Instead, we now treat the tens column as a units column, and we think of subtracting 6 from 4 and taking a 10 from the next column to make the subtraction 14 − 6.

We enter our answer of 8 (for 14 − 6) in the tens column and go to the final column, where we get an answer of 1 (for 1 − 0).

```
    1  14 13
    2̶  5̶  3̶
 -     6  7
 _____
    1  8  6
```

Subtraction in other bases is analogous to subtraction in base ten. In fact, the work will look the same, but the answers will change because the numbers represent different amounts in different bases.

base eight	base twelve	base sixteen
1 14 13	1 14 13	1 14 13
2̶ 5̶ 3̶	2̶ 5̶ 3̶	2̶ 5̶ 3̶
− 6 7	− 6 7	− 6 7
1 6 4	1 A 8	1 A C

DIRECTIONS

You are told what base is being used. Do the problem in that base and then check your work by converting to base ten. Remember that in base sixteen, we count from one through sixteen like this:

1, 2, 3, 4, 5, 6, 7, 8, 9, A, B, C, D, E, F, 10

EXAMPLE

Problem: nine, 146 − 58

Answer: base nine, 146 − 58 = 77

base ten, 123 − 53 = 70; $70_{ten} = 77_{nine}$

PROBLEMS

297. eight, 65 − 42

298. twelve, 65 − 42

299. eight, 65 − 47

300. sixteen, 65 − 47

301. sixteen, CB − AC

302. two, 10011010 − 1011001

303. four, 2122 − 1121

304. We have talked about various number bases, such as bases two, four, five, nine, and sixteen.

Can we also have a number base of

a. thirteen? Explain.

b. three? Explain.

c. one? Explain.

305. Now think about how multiplication works in base ten, and use analogous reasoning to multiply in other bases.

Make up some problems and check them out by converting to base ten.

(Don't make the problems <u>too</u> simple. We already know that $11 \times 2 = 22$ in any base greater than two. On the other hand, don't make them too hard. Who wants to check an answer to the base sixteen problem 345A6 × BF98C?)

Reference

Classroom Quickies, Books 1– 3

REARRANGE LETTERS

DIRECTIONS

Use the letters at the top to fill in the chart so that words are formed and the sentence makes sense.

A shaded space in the chart shows the end of a word. Two shaded spaces together show the end of a sentence.

Except for the last line, the end of a line is not the end of a word unless there is a shaded space there.

When you have filled in the chart, answer the question asked.

PROBLEM

306.

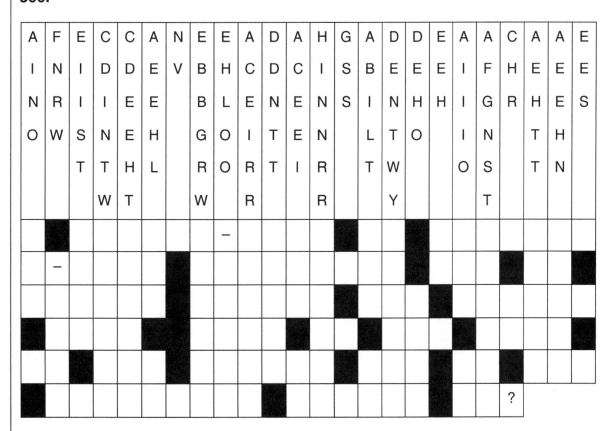

MISCELLANEOUS PROBLEMS

PROBLEMS

307. How long is one-tenth of an hour?

308. How many tenths of an hour is 36 minutes?

309. Suppose a clock showed time in hours and tenths of hours instead of in hours and minutes.

How would this clock show a time of 9:42?

310. Lawana punches in and out on a time clock where she works.

The clock punches in tenths of an hour, so if Lawana punches in at 8:06, the time card shows 8.1 (that is, 1/10 hour past 8:00).

a–c. What time will the time card show if Lawana punches in at

a. 9:12?

b. 8:48?

c. 10:00?

[Problem continued on next page.]

Reference

*Math
Word
Problems*

[Problem continued from previous page.]

d–g.   Lawana does not always punch in right on a tenth of an hour. In this case, the clock shows the next higher tenth of an hour on the time card.

For example, if Lawana punches in at 8:06, her time card will show her in at 8.1. If she punches in any time from 8:07 through 8:12, her time card will show her in at 8.2.

What time will the time card show if Lawana punches in at

d.   8:04?

e.   9:25?

f.   10 minutes before 11 o'clock?

g.   18 minutes before noon?

h–k.   A different clock is used for punching out. It, too, punches in tenths of an hour, but it punches either on the tenth of an hour or on the previous tenth.

For example, if Lawana punches out at 3:06, her time card shows her punched out at 3.1. If she punches out from 3:07 through 3:11, her card will show 3.1.

What time will Lawana's time card show if she punches out at

h.   4:19?

i.   4:59?

j.   15 minutes before 5 o'clock?

k.   6 minutes after 5 o'clock?

Reference

Inductive Thinking Skills

NUMBER PATTERNS

DIRECTIONS

For each problem, at least three parts are shown. The last part has a question mark.

Figure out what was done to the first part to get the second part. See if the same thing was done to the second part to get the third part. (If it wasn't, go back and start again.)

There is a pattern followed to get each change. Find the pattern and then use it to replace the question mark with the correct numbers.

EXAMPLE

Problem: a. 1　　　　　　　　b. 1, 2

　　　　　　c. 1, 2, 3　　　　　d. ?

Answer:　d. 1, 2, 3, 4

(What was done to part **a** to get part **b**? A comma was added, and the next number was included. What was done to part **b** to get part **c**? The same thing—a comma was added, and the next number was included. So to get part **d**, we do the same thing again—add a comma and include the next number.)

PROBLEMS

311.　a. 3×37　　　　b. 5×39

　　　c. 7×41　　　　d. ?

312.　a. 1, 10　　　　　b. 2, 9

　　　c. 3, 8　　　　　　d. ?

313.　a. 1　　　　　　　b. 3

　　　c. 6　　　　　　　d. 10

　　　e. 15　　　　　　f. ?

314. a. 1, 1   b. 1, 1, 2, 3
          c. 1, 1, 2, 3, 5, 8   d. 1, 1, 2, 3, 5, 8, 13, 21
          e. ?

315. a. 1   b. 4
          c. 27   d. 256
          e. ?

316. a. 80   b. 120
          c. 180   d. 270
          e. ?

317. a. 1 + 1 = 2   b. 2 + 2 = 4
          c. 4 + 4 = 13   d. 13 + 13 = 31
          e. 31 + 31 = 112   f. ?

318. a. 1 × 5 = 5   b. 2 × 5 = A
          c. 3 × 5 = F   d. 4 × 5 = 14
          e. ?

Reference

Basic Thinking Skills

DIRECTIONS

Copy each problem.

Each problem lists some numbers and some blanks.

Find a pattern formed by the numbers listed.

Fill in the blanks so that the pattern is continued. (You may find more than one pattern. If so, use any pattern you find.)

EXAMPLE

Problem: 1, 2, 3, 4, __, __, __, __

One answer: 1, 2, 3, 4, <u>5</u>, <u>6</u>, <u>7</u>, <u>8</u> (Here, the pattern is a simple counting pattern.)

Another answer: 1, 2, 3, 4, <u>7</u>, <u>8</u>, <u>15</u>, <u>16</u> The pattern here is: Add the first two numbers to get the next number; add 1 to get the number after that; add the two new numbers to get the third new number; add 1 to get the next number; continue in the same way.)

PROBLEMS

319.   1, 1, 2, 3, 5, 8, 13, __, __, __, __

320.   1, 2, 4, 1, 5, 10, 4, 11, __, __, __, __

321.   3, 4, 8, 5, 10, 11, 22, 19, __, __, __, __

322.   1, 2, 4, 12, 9, 5, 15, 20, __, __, __, __

323.   1, 2, 6, 3, 6, 18, 9, __, __, __, __

Reference

Algebra Word Problems— Diophantine Problems

Classroom Quickies, Books 1– 3

DIOPHANTINE PROBLEMS

PROBLEM

324. Claudine and Barry thought the meat prices they had been quoted were too high, so they looked at supermarket ads in the newspaper.

They found rolled roast for $2.60 a pound, round steak for $1.80 a pound, and boneless hams for $1.70 a pound.

There were catches here, though: the roast had to weigh at least 5 pounds, and the ham had to weigh at least 8 pounds.

They decided to buy the meat at the supermarket and to buy the chicken and fish at the store whose prices were $3 for 5 pounds of boned chicken and $3 a pound for filleted pollock.

They still want to buy 100 pounds for $100, and they still want fish, chicken, and other meat. They would like to have some each of the supermarket's three kinds of meat, but they will settle for buying only one kind if they have to.

What can they buy to get 100 pounds for $100, if the chicken has to be purchased in multiples of 5 pounds? (Figure that only whole pounds of the items are to be purchased.)

Hint: Even if they could buy 100 pounds of one thing, we know they can't buy 100 pounds of chicken, because that would take only $60. If they buy 95 pounds of chicken, that would take $57, leaving $43 to spend on 5 pounds of other things, an average $8.60 a pound, whereas the most expensive other thing is only $3 a pound. Similar reasoning brings us to see that the most chicken they can buy is 80 pounds.

Analogously, if they buy only 5 pounds of chicken, that's $3 spent, which leaves $97 to spend on 95 pounds, an average of only about $1.02 a pound. Nothing but chicken is that cheap, so they have to buy more than 5 pounds of chicken. Similar figuring will show that they must buy at least 70 pounds of chicken.

This is a tough problem! There are lots of answers.

Reference

Basic Thinking Skills

Algebra Word Problems— Diophantine Problems

MISCELLANEOUS PROBLEM

PROBLEM

325. Lincoln said, "I am thinking of a number. I can divide it by 2, 3, 4, 5, 6, or 7 without having any remainder left."

Assume that Lincoln is not lying.

a. What is the least number Lincoln can be thinking of?

b. Suppose the number Lincoln is thinking of is not the answer to part **a**.

If he divides his number by 8, might he have a remainder of 1?

If so, find the least such number.

If not, why not?

c. Same question as for part **b**, except use 9 instead of 8.

d. Same question again, except use 10 instead of 8.

e. Same question again, except use 11 instead of 8.

Reference

Classroom Quickies, Books 1– 3

WEIGHING PROBLEM

PROBLEM

326. You have six balls, all of which look exactly the same.

Four of them are normal and these four all weigh the same.

The other two weigh the same as each other but are slightly lighter or heavier than the other four.

You have a balance scale. How can you find the two odd balls in at most four weighings?

TEACHING SUGGESTIONS AND ANSWERS

INTRODUCTION

Many people assume that the critical thinking needed for mathematics automatically transfers to other subject areas. Research, however, shows that no such transfer generally occurs *unless the student is taught to think critically in a variety of contexts*.

It has also been shown that not only is there no transfer of critical thinking activity outside the subject area but that there is often no transfer *even within the subject area* unless the teacher *teaches for transfer*.

The remedy for this is to involve the student in many facets of critical thinking, both inside and outside a mathematical context, so that (s)he is likely to think critically when confronted with new information.

Consequently, many of the problems in this series do not involve mathematics per se but concentrate rather on developing various aspects of critical thinking needed for success in mathematics. These aspects include the following:

- analyzing a problem to determine a solution (rather than jumping to a conclusion)
- applying old knowledge to new situations
- arriving at a conclusion by process of elimination
- catching contradictions and inconsistencies
- deductive reasoning
- determining whether information is relevant or irrelevant
- distinguishing among possible, probable, and necessary inferences
- inductive reasoning
- learning that there may be various ways to solve a problem
- looking for a logical starting point in a problem that seems unsolvable
- organizing data so that it can be more easily used
- perceiving logical patterns
- using proof by contradiction (indirect proof)
- realizing that a problem may have more than one acceptable solution
- reasoning by analogy
- trying something to see if it works when logic doesn't suggest a solution
- weighing given information to determine truth or falsity

GENERAL INFORMATION

In some subjects, learning need not occur in a particular order. In geography, for example, knowledge about the frequency of earthquakes and other natural phenomena in country X can come before or after knowledge of X's rivers and principal industries, which, in turn, can come before or after any knowledge about country Y.

In arithmetic, however, we have a different situation. Long division comes after subtraction and multiplication, which, in turn, come after addition; division by a two-digit number comes after division by a one-digit number. Nearly every new arithmetic process learned needs application of a previous process learned thereby demanding a review of, and broadening the scope of, prior knowledge.

In recognition of the merit of review, much of the new material introduced at one level in this series is reintroduced at a higher level. With rare exceptions, however, the difficulty of the problems increases as the level increases. The exceptions occur for one of three reasons: (1) The problem has proved to be fun for various ages; (2) A relatively difficult problem is included at a lower level so that the gifted student is challenged; or (3) A relatively easy problem is included at a higher level so that the slower student has success.

Students tend to react negatively to a crowded textbook page and to give it only cursory attention in order to get through it. The result, of course, is that not much critical thinking occurs. On the other hand, the students are suspicious of a comparatively empty page and tend to concentrate on and think about the material there because they intuitively feel that it can't be as easy as it looks.

With this in mind, nearly every page in this series has a generous amount of white space, and the amount of white space on any one page is pretty much in direct proportion to the amount of thought or discussion required to solve the problems on it. In fact, sometimes only one relatively short problem appears on a page, and in these cases intuition is correct: the problem, which may or may not *look* simple, either requires a good deal of thought or has a history of needing much class discussion because different students produce different answers for it.

A few routine problems are included in some sections of this series in order to give the students practice in using a new concept, but the great majority of the problems are designed to stimulate critical thinking. Most of the pages are intended to be used as supplementary materials taking fifteen minutes or so of class time.

Problems range from relatively easy to relatively hard. To judge whether or not you think the problem is appropriate for your class, it is suggested that you do each problem yourself before assigning it.

At the bottoms of some pages are either statements or questions that have no bearing on the other material there. Some are included simply because they are interesting to think about or to know, and others are intended either as nonsense or as mild jokes.

Several of the problems in this series are similar to problems that can be found in recreational mathematics books. Such books usually have a different Dewey decimal number (793) than ordinary books on mathematics (510), but recreational problems can sometimes be found in both of these categories, as well as others. Check with your school and public librarians for their practices in numbering such books.

ARITHMETIC LEVELS OF THIS SERIES

Not all schools are able to teach an optimal arithmetic curriculum. High absenteeism, lack of parental support, and negative peer pressure can combine to frustrate the teachers' attempts to stick to the syllabus. With this in mind, the arithmetic required by the problems in this series has been geared toward the reduced syllabi.

This does not imply that the critical thinking levels of the problems have also been limited. The ages of the intended students have been considered, but otherwise it has been assumed that whatever arithmetic the students know, they are capable of thinking critically about it.

Specifically, the ages and arithmetic knowledge assumed are as follows:

BOOK 1: 8–10 years old, grades 3–4. The arithmetic assumes only the most basic knowledge of fractions (such as knowing that half of twelve is six) and includes no complicated addition or subtraction, no long multiplication or division, and no decimals, percents, or areas. Multiplication is usually limited to knowing simple facts such as $3 \times 4 = 12$. Division is similarly restricted.

BOOK 2: 10–12 years old, grades 5–6. It is assumed that the student can handle integral addition and subtraction, simple long division and multiplication, addition and subtraction of simple mixed numbers, and multiplication and division of simple fractions. With one exception, no three-digit divisors are used. No complicated fractions, percents, or areas are included. Problems involving decimals are limited to students who use hand calculators. These same problems offer alternative numbers to students who must figure by hand.

BOOK 3: 12–14 years old, grades 7–8. Reasonable facility with the four basic operations using integers or fractions is expected. Decimals rarely appear and then are limited to simple percent or money problems or to students who use hand calculators. A working knowledge (but not a profound understanding) of percents and simple areas is assumed. Some problems involve simple powers.

BOOK 4: age 14 years and older, grades 9–12. The arithmetic here expects general facility with the four basic operations on integers, fractions, and decimals, along with the ability to work reasonably well with percents and areas. Some problems involve simple powers and simple square roots. No college preparatory mathematics knowledge is expected, but some problems demand fairly complex reasoning about arithmetic.

REFERENCES

At the top left of many pages you will see the word "REFERENCE" followed by one or more titles. These titles correspond to the list below and indicate that similar material can be found in these Critical Thinking Books & Software publications.
ALGEBRA WORD PROBLEMS
    AGES AND COINS
    DIOPHANTINE PROBLEMS

TEACHING THINKING

If we are to encourage our students to think critically, we have to give them time to do so, for critical thinking entails more than simply looking at a problem and immediately knowing the answer. With this in mind, avoid doing your students' thinking for them. Encourage them to reason out the answers themselves.

Don't think you have to know all the answers. If you're really teaching your students to think critically, they'll ask many questions you won't be able to answer.

Students are proficient imitators. Show by example the way you want them to react under various conditions:

- Encourage questions, including questions about opinions you've expressed.

- Treat the students courteously and insist they be courteous to each other during a discussion. An argument can be spirited, even heated, without resorting to name-calling or other derogatory comments. Don't allow something like, "That's really a stupid thing to say!" to pass. Insist that the student who says it either apologize or back it up.

- Make learning a team effort, with yourself as part of the team.

- Don't try to fake your way. If you change your mind about an answer, tell the students, particularly if it was their arguments that convinced you. If you don't know an answer, say forthrightly, "I don't know." You might like to add something to that admission: "I wonder how we could find out?" Or, "That's beyond my education." Or, "Let me think about it and see if I can come up with an answer for tomorrow."

- Encourage class discussion, especially of different

  - viewpoints
  - ways of looking at a problem
  - ways of attacking a problem
  - answers to a problem

Some problems might be too hard for an individual student to solve and unsuitable for discussion by the full class. Try grouping the students in sets of three to five to work on these. Decide on the groupings beforehand so that you have at least one good thinker, and preferably two, in each group. Avoid grouping the best and poorest thinkers together. Have the students move their desks so that each group is a self-contained circle.

ANSWERS AND COMMENTS

Page 1

1. Other solutions are possible.

   a. The green man takes his dog over and comes back to take the purple man over. The green man stays with his dog, and the purple man returns. The purple man takes his dog across and then returns and takes the striped man across. The purple man stays, and the striped man returns for his dog.

   b. I don't see how they can.

Page 2

2. You start with ten dollars and forty-two cents. You spend fifty-nine cents plus two dollars and sixty-six cents. How much do you have left? [$10.42 − $.59 − $2.66 = $7.17]

Puzzles like this provide excellent opportunities for the students to exercise their critical thinking abilities. There are several discoveries for them to make, among which are:

1) When only one letter appears, it can be filled in.

2) When a word contains only one letter, that letter is "A" or "I." (A single letter could also be an initial—e.g., Ulysses S. Grant—but not in these particular puzzles.)

3) To make the remaining choices more obvious, used letters should be crossed off.

4) Only certain letters can be used to begin or end a two-letter word. For example, no two-letter word begins with C or R, so if the letters C, R, and T are in a column where a two-letter word begins, then T is the choice to make. The only ordinary two-letter words starting with T are TO and TV, so any other letters appearing in the next column can usually be ruled out.

5) A three-letter word starting with TH is THE or THY.

6) A three-letter word starting with Y is probably YES, YET, or YOU. A three-letter word ending with U is probably YOU.

7) A four-letter word starting with TH is probably THAT, THAN, THEM, THEN, or THEY.

8) Only certain sequences of letters are probable. For example, words don't begin or end with RW or PM (but they might begin with WR or end with MP).

Pages 3–5

3–7. $300

8. a. $60 million

   b. $63.6 million ($63,600,000)

   c. $123.6 million ($123,600,000)

   d. The counting will take about 31.7 years, so the student will be about 31 years 8 months older. For most high school students, that will put them in their late forties.

9. The method multiplies by 100 and divides by 4, giving the same result as multiplying by 25. That is, 25 = 100/4.

10. The method multiplies by 10 and divides by 2. That is, 5 = 10/2.

Page 6

11. 5,865,696,000,000 miles (hand); 5,878,603,375,920 miles (calculator)

12. For the computation by hand, there are 24 ⑨ 365 = 8,760 hours in a year, so the space ship would travel 8,760,000,000 miles in that time. Then the answer is 5,865,696,000,000 ÷ 8,760,000,000 = 669 3/5 years. For the calculator users, the space ship would travel 1,000,000 × 24 × 365.25 = 8,766,000,000 miles in a year, so one light year would take 5,878,603,375,920 ÷ 8,766,000,000 = 670.61412 years ≈ 670 3/5 years.

13. a. 25,222,492,800,000 (hand); 25,277,994,516,456 (calculator)

    b. 4.3 years

Stress to the students that a light-year is a measure of distance, not a measure of time. Once they have grasped this concept, questions about time (e.g., "How long does it take for light to reach Earth from

Proxima Centauri?") may confuse them, and it may take several examples of analogous problems to clarify the situation.

Suggested examples include:

- You want to go 100 miles (distance). How long will it take (time) if you go at 50 mph (rate)?
- A racehorse ran at an average speed of 30 mph (rate). How long did it take (time) for the horse to go around a 1-mile track (distance)?
- Your friend's house is 264 feet away (distance). If you run all the way at 15 mph (rate), how many seconds (time) will it take you to get there?
- The sun is 93,000,000 miles away (distance). Light travels at 186,000 miles a second (rate). How long does it take the sun's light to reach us?
- Proxima Centauri is 4.3 light-years away (distance). Light travels at 186,282 miles a second (rate). How long does it take light from Proxima Centauri to reach Earth?

Encourage the students to use hand calculators for these problems. They will have to use their critical thinking abilities to figure out how to get the calculator to do the required work when the numbers to be entered or the answers are beyond the calculator's capacity. (If the problem requires division, and if the divisor has more digits—not counting trailing zeros—than the calculator's capacity, allow the divisor to be rounded off.)

If the students do not have calculators available, they can use 186,000 miles a second for the speed of light and 365 days for a year. Answers below are given both ways.

Page 7

14. a. 143,077 miles a second

b. 124,000 miles a second

c. 77,500 miles a second

15. Not in our known universe, since it is believed that light never moves faster than when in a vacuum and that nothing moves faster than light. (However, scientists have hypothesized that if particles of superluminal velocities, called tachyons, did exist, they would have imaginary masses—i.e., some ordinary value

times $\sqrt{-1}$. Although there is no evidence to indicate that tachyons exist, neither is there evidence to show that they do not exist.)

Page 8

16. a. 76.9%

b. 66.7%

c. 41.7%

See if the students realize that they get the same answer whether they divide 1 by the index of refraction, or whether they divide the speed of light through the medium by 186,000.

Page 9

17. The first line shows the numbers of gallons the jugs hold. Successive lines show how many gallons are in each jug. Other solutions are possible.

11	7	4	
11	0	0	Start
4	7	0	
4	3	4	
8	3	0	
8	0	3	
1	7	3	
1	6	4	
5	6	0	

Nothing is better than complete happiness in life, and a school cafeteria meal is better than nothing.

Pages 10–12

How often have we seen outlandish answers to mathematical problems? For example, a student gets an answer of 45 to the problem 45 × 9, because, "Everyone knows that 0 is nothing, so 45 is the same as 405." (Yet the same student will readily agree that $405 is not at all the same as $45.) Or a student adds three numbers, each of which is between 10 and 20, and is not at all disturbed when his or her answer is not between 30 and 60. It sometimes seems as though such students suspect that mathematics has something to do with magic, in which case, they reason, one answer should be as good as another.

There are various degrees of likelihood to be considered when choosing whether or not to accept something. Among these are: fact; highly probable; more likely than not; fifty-fifty; possible but not probable; possible but unlikely; impossible. Wishful thinking and fantasy probably come (usually) somewhere between the last two.

It is important that students learn to think about given information and to distinguish among the various degrees of likelihood. As a first step toward this goal, the two problems following are designed to press the student to make relatively easy decisions about likelihood. Each case is a matter of deciding simply whether a story falls within the bounds of reasonable possibility or whether it falls so far outside these bounds that it becomes mere wishful thinking or fantasy.

Pages 11–12

18. a. true to life

    b. true to life

    c. fantasy (He'd never agree to it without seeing her run or seeing how she stands up to the rigorous training needed.)

    d. true to life (Fantastic, but not quite fantasy. The editor may be running a series of articles on outstanding high school athletes.)

    e. fantasy (The Stanford man wouldn't decide such a thing without having a personal interview with Katina.)

19. a. true to life

    b. true to life

    c. fantasy

    d. fantasy

    e. true to life

    f. fantasy

    g. fantasy (It is important that the students acknowledge the fantasy in this story, for it appears to summarize the wishful thinking of some of them. It is true that an mathematics lesson may be understood when a previous one was not, but in such a case one of two things will be true, both of which were denied in the story: either the new lesson will clear up the confusion about the

previous lesson, or the new lesson will not be based on knowledge taught by the previous lesson.)

Pages 13–14

20. a–d. No. It does not disagree with the statement.

    e. Yes

    f. No. It questions the statement but doesn't disagree with it.

    g. No. It does not disagree with the statement.

    h. No. It is a specific example and it contradicts the given statement, but it is false, for 6 is not a prime number.

On page 13, your students should deduce from the last example (no bulldog is green) and from the last paragraph that a statement might be proved false in several ways, of which finding a counterexample is just one. Working on the principle that there will be at least one student who hasn't made the inference, however, you'd better mention it to the class.

Make sure the students know what is meant by a prime number, an even number, and an odd number.

Pages 15–18

21. a. Yes

    b. Yes

    c. No

    d. No

    e. No

    f. No

    g. Yes

    h. No

    i. Yes

22. a. No. This doesn't relate to the statement.

    b. No. This discusses its usefulness, rather than whether or not it should be allowed.

    c. No. The fact that he won't permit it does not imply that he shouldn't permit it.

23. a. No. This supports the statement.

    b. No. The statement is about notably intelligent people, so the neighbor is not a counterexample. (Those who thought this was a counterexample have mistaken the converse of the proposition for the proposition. The proposition says, in effect, "If a person is intelligent, then that person has a sense of humor." The converse of this says, "If someone has a sense of humor, then that person is intelligent." We see that statement **b** is a counterexample to the converse of the given statement but not to the statement itself.)

c. Yes

24. No. This kind of statement has no counterexample.

25. No. This kind of statement has no counterexample.

26. a. No. Aside from the fact that no example is given, this discusses whether or not someone <u>will</u> agree, rather than whether or not someone <u>should</u> agree, to give a job to any teenager who wants one.

b. Yes

Pages 19–20

27. No. A counterexample is an example that proves a (general) statement to be false, so there can be no counterexample to a true statement.

28. For this problem, encourage the students to think of a set of two statements to use as a model. That is, the two given statements are in the form, "All [word or phrase #1] are [word or phrase #2]. I found a [#1] that is not a [#2]." The questions become less abstract if the students substitute meaningful words or phrases for #1 and #2. Their chosen first statement should be true for some, but not all, cases.

a. Yes

b. Yes

c. No. All zoffers except the one you found may be middigs.

d. Yes

e. Same as (**c**).

f. Yes

g. No

h. No

i. No. You've proved that a zoffer doesn't have to be a middig, but not the converse. For example, put zoffers = numbers that can be written as fractions, and put middigs = numbers that can be written as whole numbers. Then the statement reads, "All numbers that can be written as fractions are numbers that can be written as whole numbers." The statement can be disproved by producing the fraction 2/3, but that doesn't prove that some whole numbers cannot be written as fractions.

29. For this problem, too, encourage the students to think of a set of statements to use as a model. It will be helpful if the statement is itself true but has a false converse.

a. No. Consider the statement "All squares are four-sided figures." Finding a 3×5 rectangle is not a counterexample to the statement.

b. No

c. No

d. No

e. No

f. No

g. No

h. No

i. No

j. Yes

Although the general rule in this textbook is to include only as much on one page as the students should be expected to learn or solve in one session, these two pages of problems do not follow that rule. There are several items on each page, and it would probably be a good idea to expect a saturation point to be reached before a page is completed and to plan to end the session at that point and then come back to the remaining items another day.

Pages 21–28

Students too often make unwarranted assumptions about what they're reading or being told. A painless way to show them that they do this is to supply them with a short story and some conclusions about a subject that is simple to understand, emotionally neutral, and interesting enough to argue about.

Fairy tales and nursery rhymes not only meet these criteria but have the added advantage of being so familiar that the students are doubly likely to allow past impressions of the story to influence their interpretations of what they are now reading.

Use class discussion to decide on the answers. For each answer, ask first, "How many chose 'true'? How many 'false'? How many 'can't tell'?" and write the numbers on the chalkboard. Ask, "Who wants to start? Tell us which answer you chose and why you think it's right." Try to keep out of the discussion yourself. Let the students argue about it until they are all convinced of the same answer. It will take longer to settle without your intervention, but it will be more effective in developing the students' abilities to think critically.

Don't take for granted that my answers have to be right. I once used the same problem for three different classes, went to the first class *knowing* my answer was right, changed my mind because of the students' arguments, and changed my mind twice more because of the arguments of the students in the other two classes.

Don't think your students too old for nursery rhymes and fairy tales. My students were tenth-through twelfth-graders whose abilities ranged from gifted to educable mentally retarded and whose social inclinations ranged from aggressive gang members to shy loners. Despite the ages of the students and the numerous classes exposed to such materials, there were only a handful of times when a student objected to the first problem with a disparaging, "Hey, we're a little old for this kind of stuff, aren't we?" In each case, I said to the class after obviously considering the student's comment, "You could be right at that. I'll tell you what. I'll make a deal with you. If you'll all read the story to your-selves and decide on the first five answers without talking to anyone about them, and if we all agree on the answers, we won't do any more of the problem, and we'll move on to something else." The students thought this fair enough and set to work. It some-times took two class periods (55 minutes each) to agree on the first answer, and that was the end of any objections.

Pages 21–28

30. a. T

b. ?

c. ?. We know that she screamed in time to be rescued, but we don't know why she screamed or whether or not she recognized the wolf.

d. T

e. ?

f. ?. Maybe she forgot and left the basket at home.

g. T

h. T

i. ?

j. F

k. T

l. ?. We're told that Red didn't recognize the wolf but not that she thought the wolf was her grandmother. Maybe she thought the wolf was a friend who'd stopped by to visit.

m. F. She may or may not have been in a hurry, but she *could* have been.

n. ?. She screamed in time to be rescued, but we don't know whether or not she was rescued at all.

o. ?. Maybe he was deaf.

p. ?. He disposed of her, which could mean he tied and gagged her and hid her someplace.

31. a. ?

b. F. The first time the witch is called "a" witch and could have been any witch, but she is later called "the" witch, which means (since we're told good English is used) that we know which witch is meant.

c–d. ?. Maybe the witch thought the mother would have to show the girl how to use the spinning wheel and wanted the mother to be the one who was pricked so that she would fall asleep and the witch could steal the daughter while the father was at work.

e. T

f. ?. Probably true, but maybe it was after midnight by the time the daughter un-wrapped the spinning wheel and set it up to work with it.

g–j. ?

k. T

l. ?

32. a. T

b. F

c. F

d. ?

e. T

f. T

g. ?

h. T

i. F

j. ?

k. ?

l. T

m. F

Pages 29–47

Many of us are used to calling a mathematical function, say addition, an "operation," and this terminology is correct. However, a function is an operator as well as an operation. The symbol used to denote the function, say +, is also an operator.

As a point of interest, computer programming manuals consistently refer to mathematical functions as "operators" rather than "operations," and their symbols used as operators include not only +, – , * (multiplication), and / (division), but grouping characters such as ( ) and (( )), logical operators such as NOT, AND and OR, and conditional operators such as < and <= (less than or equal to).

Rather than call, say, addition, an operation and call its symbol, +, an operator, it is consistent with modern usage and less confusing to the students to say "operator" for both the operation and its symbol.

The order of precedence stated in the textbook is followed both in mathematics and in computer programming.

The operators ( ), [ ], { }, ×, ÷, /, +, and – , as well as exponentiation (raising to a power) and taking square roots, are discussed. The computations involved, while sometimes complex, do not result in large numbers and so do not require the use of a hand calculator.

For the grouping symbols ( ), [ ], and { }, you will notice, in the textbook Examples as well as in the

Answers in this manual, that the outer symbols are not "reduced" when the inner symbols have been eliminated. For example, the solution of

$$24 - [18/(4 + 5) + 10] = ?$$

is shown as

$$24 - [18/(4 + 5) + 10] = 24 - [18/9 + 10] = 24 - [2 + 10] = 24 - 12 = 12.$$

Some current mathematics textbooks are following computer programming practice by using only ( ). In that case, the problem shown here would be written as

$$24 - (18/(4 + 5) + 10).$$

I'm as likely as not to write the problem that way when working on my own, but the students generally find it confusing. As a result, all three of ( ), [ ], and { } are used in this textbook.

Although a common practice is to reduce the order of the remaining symbols when a lower-ranking symbol has been eliminated—e.g., change the [ ] to ( ) and change the { } to [ ] once the original ( ) is gone—this, too, results in confusing some students. Furthermore, I don't see any purpose in doing it. Consequently, the grouping symbols that the problem starts with are the symbols that are used throughout the solution.

It is assumed that the students know what is meant by expressions such as 2^3 and $\sqrt{9}$.

Pages 29–33

Answers will vary.

33. $4 + 8 - 12 = 12 - 12 = 0$

34. $12 - 8 - \sqrt{4} = 12 - 8 - 2 = 4 - 2 = 2$

35. $8 \times \sqrt{4} - 12 = 8 \times 2 - 12 = 16 - 12 = 4$

36. $8 - 12/4 = 8 - 3 = 5$

37. $12 \times 4/8 = 48/8 = 6$

38. $12 - 8/4 = 12 - 2 = 10$

39. $8 + \sqrt{4 + 12} = 8 + \sqrt{16} = 8 + 4 = 12$

40. $12 + 8/4 = 12 + 2 = 14$

41. $12 + 8 - \sqrt{4} = 12 + 8 - 2 = 20 - 2 = 18$

Stress the importance of working from left to right. Although it doesn't matter for addition and multiplication because they are associative, subtraction and division are not associative, and most students won't stop and think about this if they feel like starting at some point other than the left end. As examples, 24/4/2 = (24/4)/2 ≠ 24/(4/2), and 10 − 5 − 4 = (10 − 5) − 4 ≠ 10 − (5 − 4).

Insist that the students show their work so that you can verify their reasoning.

Pages 34–36

42. 24/(6 − 2) + (7 − 3) × 5 = 24/4 + (7 − 3) × 5 = 24/4 + 4 × 5 = 6 + 4 × 5 = 6 + 20 = 26.

43. 8×3^2 − [21/(5 − 2) + 5 × 11] = 8×3^2 − [21/3 + 5 × 11] = 8×3^2 − [7 + 5 × 11] = 8×3^2 − [7 + 55] = 8×3^2 − 62 = 8 × 9 − 62 = 72 − 62 = 10

44. 26 − [$(9 − 5)^2$ + 6] = 26 − [4^2 + 6] = 26 − [16 + 6] = 26 − 22 = 4

45. 6 × 7 − ($\sqrt{25}$ + 48/4/3) = 6 × 7 − (5 + 48/4/3) = 6 × 7 − (5 + 12/3) = 6 × 7 − (5 + 4) = 6 × 7 − 9 = 42 − 9 = 33

46. $\sqrt{4}^3$ × (1 + 2 × 3) = $\sqrt{4}^3$ × (1 + 6) = $\sqrt{4}^3$ × 7 = 2^3 × 7 = 8 × 7 = 56

47. 88 − {4 + 5 × [3 + 45/(7 + 2)]} = 88 − {4 + 5 × [3 + 45/9]} = 88 − {4 + 5 × [3 + 5]} = 88 − {4 + 5 × 8} = 88 − {4 + 40} = 88 − 44 = 44

48. $48/2^3/2$ + 4 × 5 − (20 − 2 × 8) = $48/2^3/2$ + 4 × 5 − (20 − 16) = $48/2^3/2$ + 4 × 5 − 4 = 48/8/2 + 4 × 5 − 4 = 6/2 + 4 × 5 − 4 = 3 + 4 × 5 − 4 = 3 + 20 − 4 = 23 − 4 = 19

49. 58 − {5 + 2 × 4 − [3 × 12 − (4 × 5 + 14)] + 2} = 58 − {5 + 2 × 4 − [3 × 12 − (20 + 14)] + 2} = 58 − {5 + 2 × 4 − [3 × 12 − 34] + 2} = 58 − {5 + 2 × 4 − [36 − 34] + 2} = 58 − {5 + 2 × 4 − 2 + 2} = 58 − {5 + 8 − 2 + 2} = 58 − {13 − 2 + 2} = 58 − {11 + 2} = 58 − 13 = 45

50. 3^3 − (2^4 + $\sqrt{25}$ + $\sqrt{49}$ − 1) = 3^3 − (16 + $\sqrt{25}$ + $\sqrt{49}$ − 1) = 3^3 − (16 + 5 + $\sqrt{49}$ − 1) = 3^3 − (16 + 5 + 7 − 1) = 3^3 − (21 + 7 − 1) = 3^3 − (28 − 1) = 3^3 − 27 = 27 − 27 = 0

51. $(2 \times 3 + 4)^2$ + $\sqrt{49}$ × 2^3 − 1 − 5 × [(9 × 5 − 1)/4] − 3^2 × (7 + 4) = $(6 + 4)^2$ + $\sqrt{49}$ × 2^3 − 1 − 5 × [(9 × 5 − 1)/4] − 3^2 × (7 + 4) =

10^2 + $\sqrt{49}$ × 2^3 − 1 − 5 × [(9 × 5 − 1)/4] − 3^2 × (7 + 4) =

10^2 + $\sqrt{49}$ × 2^3 − 1 − 5 × [(45 − 1)/4] − 3^2 × (7 + 4) =

10^2 + $\sqrt{49}$ × 2^3 − 1 − 5 × [44/4] − 3^2 × (7 + 4) =

10^2 + $\sqrt{49}$ × 2^3 − 1 − 5 × [44/4] − 3^2 × 11 =

10^2 + $\sqrt{49}$ × 2^3 − 1 − 5 × 11 − 3^2 × 11 =

100 + $\sqrt{49}$ × 2^3 − 1 − 5 × 11 − 3^2 × 11 =

100 + 7 × 2^3 − 1 − 5 × 11 − 3^2 × 11 =

100 + 7 × 8 − 1 − 5 × 11 − 3^2 × 11 =

100 + 7 × 8 − 1 − 5 × 11 − 9 × 11 =

100 + 56 − 1 − 5 × 11 − 9 × 11 =

100 + 56 − 1 − 55 − 9 × 11 =

100 + 56 − 1 − 55 − 99 =

156 − 1 − 55 − 99 = 155 − 55 − 99 = 100 − 99 = 1

52. $\{9^2$ − (3 × 5 − 4) − $[8^2$ − (5 + 7) × 2]} × {19 − [$(\sqrt{3 + 13})^2$ + 1]} =

$\{9^2$ − (15 − 4) − $[8^2$ − (5 + 7) × 2]} × {19 − [$(\sqrt{3 + 13})^2$ + 1]} =

$\{9^2$ − 11 − $[8^2$ − (5 + 7) × 2]} × {19 − [$(\sqrt{3 + 13})^2$ + 1]} =

$\{9^2$ − 11 − $[8^2$ − 12 × 2]} × {19 − [$(\sqrt{3 + 13})^2$ + 1]} =

$\{9^2$ − 11 − $[8^2$ − 12 × 2]} × {19 − [$(\sqrt{16})^2$ + 1]} =

$\{9^2$ − 11 − $[8^2$ − 12 × 2]} × {19 − [4^2 + 1]} =

$\{9^2$ − 11 − [64 − 12 × 2]} × {19 − [4^2 + 1]} =

$\{9^2$ − 11 − [64 − 24]} × {19 − [4^2 + 1]} =

$\{9^2$ − 11 − 40} × {19 − [4^2 + 1]} =

$\{9^2$ − 11 − 40} × {19 − [16 + 1]} =

$\{9^2$ − 11 − 40} × {19 − 17} = {81 − 11 − 40} × {19 − 17} =

{70 − 40} × {19 − 17} = 30 × {19 − 17} = 30 × 2 = 60

You will want to be able to follow the students' reasoning, so make sure they show their work. In actual practice, we don't usually show as much detail as is shown in the lesson Examples and in the answers below. Instead, we do all equivalent operations at the same time. For instance, the first answer below would be more likely to look like this:

24/(6 − 2) + (7 − 3) × 5 = 24/4 + 4 × 5 = 6 + 20 = 26

The detail is shown, however, so that there is no question about the order in which the computations are to be done.

Pages 37–39

Make sure the students show their work step by step, as in the answers below.

53. $(5 + 3) \times 2 - (4 + 1) = 8 \times 2 - (4 + 1) = 8 \times 2 - 5 = 16 - 5 = 11$

54. $4^2 - (2 + 3) \times 3 = 4^2 - 5 \times 3 = 16 - 5 \times 3 = 16 - 15 = 1$

55. $4 \times 11 + 3 + 2 \times 5 - 6 = 44 + 3 + 2 \times 5 - 6 = 44 + 3 + 10 - 6 = 47 + 10 - 6 = 57 - 6 = 51$

56. $17 - [25 - (1 + 3) \times 5] = 17 - [25 - 4 \times 5] = 17 - [25 - 20] = 17 - 5 = 12$

57. $48/(3^2 - 1) + (7 - 5) \times 6 = 48/(9 - 1) + (7 - 5) \times 6 = 48/8 + (7 - 5) \times 6 = 48/8 + 2 \times 6 = 6 + 2 \times 6 = 6 + 12 = 18$

58. $36/(3 \times 12/4)/2 = 36/(36/4)/2 = 36/9/2 = 4/2 = 2$

59. $[5 \times (3 + 2 \times 3) - 5^2] \times 5 = [5 \times (3 + 6) - 5^2] \times 5 = [5 \times 9 - 5^2] \times 5 = [5 \times 9 - 25] \times 5 = [45 - 25] \times 5 = 20 \times 5 = 100$

60. $39/[(5^2 - 4^2)/3] - 2 \times 5 = 39/[(25 - 4^2)/3] - 2 \times 5 = 39/[(25 - 16)/3] - 2 \times 5 = 39/[9/3] - 2 \times 5 = 39/3 - 2 \times 5 = 13 - 2 \times 5 = 13 - 10 = 3$

61. $3 \times 5 \times [7 + (5 + 4) \times 6 + 7 - 6 \times 11] = 3 \times 5 \times [7 + 9 \times 6 + 7 - 6 \times 11] = 3 \times 5 \times [7 + 54 + 7 - 6 \times 11] = 3 \times 5 \times [7 + 54 + 7 - 66] = 3 \times 5 \times [61 + 7 - 66] = 3 \times 5 \times [68 - 66] = 3 \times 5 \times 2 = 15 \times 2 = 30$

62. $[(10 - 7) \times 4 - 2] \times (3^2 - 2^3) - 4 = [3 \times 4 - 2] \times (3^2 - 2^3) - 4 = [3 \times 4 - 2] \times (9 - 2^3) - 4 = [3 \times 4 - 2] \times (9 - 8) - 4 = [3 \times 4 - 2] \times 1 - 4 = [12 - 2] \times 1 - 4 = 10 \times 1 - 4 = 10 - 4 = 6$

63. $7 \times [158 - 2 - 7 \times (6 + 2) - 3 \times 5^2 - 2 \times 9 + 1] = 7 \times [158 - 2 - 7 \times 8 - 3 \times 5^2 - 2 \times 9 + 1] = 7 \times [158 - 2 - 7 \times 8 - 3 \times 25 - 2 \times 9 + 1] = 7 \times [158 - 2 - 56 - 3 \times 25 - 2 \times 9 + 1] = 7 \times [158 - 2 - 56 - 75 - 2 \times 9 + 1] = 7 \times [158 - 2 - 56 - 75 - 18 + 1] = 7 \times [156 - 56 - 75 - 18 + 1] = 7 \times [100 - 75 - 18 + 1] = 7 \times [25 - 18 + 1] = 7 \times [7 + 1] = 7 \times 8 = 56$

Page 40

64. Algebra:

a. $(r - s) - t = (r - 1s) - 1t = [r + (-1)s] + (-1)t =$ (associative property of addition) $r + [(-1)s + (-1)t] =$ (distributive property) $r + (-1)[s + t] = r - 1[s + t] = r - (s + t)$.

b. $r - (s - t) = r - 1[1s - 1t] = r + (-1)[1s + (-1)t] =$ (distributive property) $r + [(-1)s + 1t] =$ (associative property of addition) $[r + (-1)s] + 1t = (r - s) + t$.

c. $(r - s) + t = [r + (-1)s] + t =$ (associative property of addition) $r + [(-1)s + t] =$ (commutative property of addition) $r + [t + (-1)s] =$ (associative property of addition) $(r + t) + (-1)s = (r + t) - s$.

d. $r - s - t =$ (part **a** above) $r - (s + t) =$ (commutative property of addition) $r - (t + s) =$ (part **a** above) $r - t - s$.

Students: Call the three numbers #1, #2, and #3.

a. Suppose we take #1 and subtract #2 from it and then subtract #3 from that answer. Then we've reduced #1 by both of the other two, which means we've reduced it by the sum of the other two. This shows that (#1 − #2) − #3 = #1 − (#2 + #3).

b. Suppose we subtract #3 from #2. Then #2 has been reduced by the amount of #3. Now when we subtract that result from #1, we're subtracting less (by the amount of #3) than we would if we subtracted (from #1) #2 without reducing it first. So if we subtract all of #2 from #1, we subtract more (by the amount of #3) than we should, and we have to add #3 to the result in order to make the final answer correct. This shows that #1 − (#2 − #3) = (#1 − #2) + #3.

c. Suppose we subtract #2 from #1 and then add #3 to that result. We get the same final answer as if we add #3 to #1 and then subtract #2 from that result, because in both cases #1 has been reduced by #2 but increased by #3. In other words, #1 has been changed by the amount of the difference between #2 and #3. (#1 has increased if #3 > #2, decreased if #2 > #3.) This shows that (#1 − #2) + #3 = (#1 + #3) − #2.

d. Starting with #1, whether we subtract #2 and then #3, or we subtract #3 and then #2, either way we're subtracting the sum of #2 and #3, so the order doesn't matter. So #1 − #2 − #3 = #1 − #3 − #2.

These are not easy problems for the ordinary general math student. By trying several examples, the student will be able to see that each statement is true but will probably have difficulty verbalizing it.

Two proofs are given for each problem. "Algebra" shows the proof that might be done by a student who understands elementary algebra. "Students" shows the kind of proof that the student who doesn't understand algebra might think of.

Pages 41–42

65. There are many ways to get answers. A quick run-through found solutions for all but five of the whole numbers from 0 through 100. I did not find solutions for 53, 74, 89, 95, or 99. Of the ninety-six solutions found, seven used one or both of decimals and square roots, and two used summation signs (Σ). There may, of course, be simpler solutions for those I solved, as well as solutions for the five problems I didn't solve.

66. As in the preceding set of problems, there are many correct answers. A quick run-through for this current set found solutions for all whole numbers from 0 through 100. No summation signs (Σ) were used this time. It was not necessary to use either decimals or square roots for the first fifty problems, but I used one or both of these in at least twenty-five of the last fifty-one problems. There may, of course, be simpler solutions for several of the problems in the last half.

These problems provide an admirable way to meet several teaching goals:

- Students do drill work but feel as though they're taking a break.

- The problems are open-ended in two ways: first, there is no guarantee of a solution for any given problem; second, there may be many solutions to a given problem.

- The problems require creative thinking, for there are numerous possible combinations that can be tried (most of which won't work) in order to get an answer.

- The problems demand critical thinking, because each time a combination is tried it must be analyzed and either accepted or rejected. If it is rejected, the student then must try to

figure out what is wrong with it and what needs to be changed in order to make the result acceptable.

- The problems provide a gentle way for the students to learn that (1) not all arithmetic problems have solutions, and (2) for some problems that have solutions, these solutions may have to be found by trial and error and a process of elimination.

- Even though finding a particular answer may take several minutes, the students do not react to their temporary lack of success with a loss of self-confidence, for they understand what is to be done, and they know how to go about doing it.

- The problems present an agreeable challenge. Students enjoy trying to find answers and are likely to spend some of their free time trying to do the problems.

If your students like competition, you could issue a challenge to see who can come up with the greatest number of correct answers for a given problem. For example, $6 = (3 \times 4) \div (1 \times 2) = (4 \times 3) \div (1 \times 2) = \ldots = 1 + 3 + 4 - 2 = 3 + 1 + 4 - 2 = \ldots = 12/4 + 3 =$ other combinations, too. Or the challenge could be to see who can find solutions for the longest list of numbers. If you decide on this one, it would probably be a good idea to set an upper limit, say 50 or 100. Otherwise, you're likely to be faced with computations such as 32×41 and 34^{12}.

Some of the more inventive students may come up with solutions such as

$$1 = 1^{234} \text{ and } 1 = \sum_{n=1}^{2} (n + 3 - 4$$

Pages 43–47

67. $18 > 17$; true

68. $33 \leq 27$; false

69. $24 \leq 24$; true

70. $36 \not< 20$; true

71. $9 \not\geq 18$; true

72. $55 - 25 = 30 \not\geq 30$; false

73. $16 \neq 16$; false

74. $4 \times 7 = 28 <> 24$; true

75. $8 \leq 9$; true

76. $81 \leq 64$; false

77. $20 + 55 = 75$; $3 \times 12 + 10 = 36 + 10 = 46$; $75 > 46$

78. $28 - 3 \times 7 = 28 - 21 = 7$; $49 - 5 \times 9 = 49 - 45 = 4$; $7 \ngtr 4$

79. $36/3 + 8 = 12 + 8 = 20$; $35 - 3 \times 5 = 35 - 15 = 20$; $20 = 20$

80. $4 \times 5 + 6 = 20 + 6 = 26$; $3 \times 12 - 14 = 36 - 14 = 22$; $26 \ngtr 22$; $26 \geq 22$

81. $70 - 4 \times 5 = 70 - 20 = 50$; $2 \times 5^2 = 2 \times 25 = 50$; $50 \leq 50$

82. $4 \times 5 = 20$; $60 - 40/8 - 5 \times 11 = 60 - 5 - 55 = 0$; $20 \nless 0$; $20 \neq 0$

83. $4 + 5 \times [24/(2 + 6) + 1] = 4 + 5 \times [24/8 + 1] = 4 + 5 \times 4 = 24$; $3 \times 5 - (24/4 + 6) = 15 - (6 + 6) = 15 - 12 = 3$; $24 \geq 3$; $24 \ngtr 3$

84. $[24/(5 + 1) + 2]/3 = [24/6 + 2]/3 = [4 + 2]/3 = 6/3 = 2$; $4 \times 8 - (3 \times 5 + 10) = 32 - (15 + 10) = 32 - 25 = 7$; $2 \neq 7$; $2 \ngtr 7$

Make sure the students understand that the slash through $\geq$ (or $\leq$) negates both $>$ (or $<$) and $=$. When we say that $\ngtr$ means "not greater than or equal to," we know that we mean "not greater-than-or-equal-to," but a listener might take this to mean "not greater-than or equal to"—i.e. $\ngtr$ or $=$.

Pages 48–54

Many students seem to take for granted that almost anything said during a discussion has a bearing on the topic. They assume that if a comment touches on a peripheral issue, then it is germane to the subject at hand. This is evidenced by their thinking, say, that an assignment to write a theme on "Why I Like Dogs" is satisfied by a theme on "Why I Like Dogs Better Than Cats."

The ability to differentiate between relevant and irrelevant thoughts is vital to critical thinking in mathematics. When we are doing a three-column addition problem, for instance, it doesn't do much good to think about how multiplication of fractions is done, but it does help to think about how a two-

column addition problem is done and to apply the same principles here.

Use class discussion for these problems. Although the directions don't ask for reasons for the answers, ask the students why they chose their answers. Their reasons will help clarify the difference between relevant and irrelevant comments both for themselves and their classmates.

Pages 49–54

85. a. Y
b. Y
c. N
d. Y
e. N
f. N
g. Y
h. N
i. N
j. Y

86. a. Y
b. Y (This narrows the possibilities.)
c. Y
d. N
e. Y
f. N
g. Y, but not very practical for this case.
h. Y
i. N
j. N, but it's an excellent suggestion.
k. N
l. N
m. N, but it's a good idea.

87. a. N
b. Y
c. Y
d. N
e. Y
f. Y
g. N. This has already been invented.

h. Y

i. N

j. Y or N, depending on whether or not you think such an invention is needed.

Pages 55–57

88. A. a. The border takes 2 in. from each side of the given rectangle, reducing both width and length by 4 in., so the inner rectangle, 5 in. × 8 in., has an area of 40 sq in.

   b. The easy way to figure the border's area is to take the difference in areas of the outer and inner rectangles: 108 sq in. − 40 sq in. = 68 sq in.

   B. a. The border adds 2 in. to each side of the given rectangle, so the outer rectangle, 13 in. × 16 in., has an area of 208 sq in.

   b. 208 sq in. − 108 sq in. = 100 sq in.

89. In every case, the area between the two circles is the difference between the areas of the two circles. Whether or not the circles are concentric makes no difference, so the answers to parts **A** and **B** are the same.

The radii of circles #1–4 are, respectively, 10, 9, 8, and 7 inches, so the areas are (in sq in.) 100π, 81π, 64π, and 49π. In case you did decide to countermand my instruction, the answers are given four ways: using π, and using for π 3 1/7, 3.14, and 3.1416. All answers are understood to be square inches.

a. 19π; 59 5/7; 59.66; 59.6904

b. 15π; 47 1/7; 47.10; 47.1240

c. 36π; 113 1/7; 113.04; 113.0976

d. 51π; 160 2/7; 160.14; 160.2216

e. 32π; 100 4/7; 100.48; 100.5312

Unless they have seen this kind of problem before, some of the students will have no idea of how to go about finding the answers. Aside from suggesting that they sketch a picture, or figure, for each problem, it is recommended that you not tell them how to do these problems. These are good problems for developing critical thinking ability.

For problem 89 on pages 56–57, I thought that telling the students to use the symbol for pi, rather than pi's numeric value, might allow them to con-

centrate more on how to solve the problems than o the arithmetic involved. If you feel that an answer o say, 19π sq in., doesn't have much meaning for the students, feel free to countermand my instruction.

Page 58

90. Inserting a decimal point just before the last digit is equivalent to dividing by 10, so the method uses 1/5 = 2/10. That is, instead of dividing by 5, it multiplies by 1/5.

   Probably a 0-sided figure, if such a thing could exist. It's really a nine-sided polygon.

Page 59

91. They should buy 93 pounds of chicken ($62), pounds of rolled roast ($14), and 3 pounds of salmon ($24).

This is a typical Diophantine problem. If we try to solve this problem by straight algebra, we'll have three variables but only two equations—a setup tha has an infinite number of solutions. However, a Diophantine problem has built-in conditions that lim the number of solutions. For example, Claudine and Barry can't buy a negative number of pounds of chicken, and the problem states that they don't buy any fractional pounds.

The mathematics needed for a *formal* solution of a Diophantine problem is beyond the knowledge of a general mathematics student, but such students nevertheless enjoy trying to solve the problems.

A side benefit of presenting the students with Diophantine problems is that the students learn that not all problems are as straightforward as they sound and that such problems can be solved by tria and error.

There are three more Diophantine problems in this textbook.

For information about how to solve Diophantine problems (which may be helpful to you but not to your general math students), as well as for more Diophantine problems to give your students, see the booklet *Diophantine Problems* in the ALGEBRA WORD PROBLEMS series.

Page 60

92. When we travel eastward through time zones, we add an hour for each zone until we cross the international date line, when we subtract

one day—i.e., 24 hours. Notice that Sydney's time is 18 hours later than Los Angeles' time and 15 hours later than New York City's time. Traveling eastward from either Los Angeles or New York City, we don't cross the international date line before reaching Australia. (And, of course, if we travel eastward to Australia, then it is farther from Los Angeles than from New York City.)

But if we travel westward, we subtract one hour for each time zone until we cross the international date line, at which point we add one day. If we start west from Los Angeles at, say 2:00 A.M. Monday, we will cross time zones of 1:00 A.M. Monday, 12:00 A.M. Monday, and 11:00 P.M. Sunday, and instead of going to 10:00 P.M. of Sunday, we will cross the international date line and add one day, making it 10:00 P.M. Monday. Our next time zone will be 9:00 P.M. Monday, and the one after that will be Sydney's time zone, 8:00 P.M. Monday.

In other words, Sydney is only 6 time zones westward from Los Angles (9 from New York City). This shows that Sydney is closer to Los Angeles than to New York City. Notice that if we can take time zones as an approximately accurate gauge of distance, then going westward is only about 1/3 as far as going eastward from Los Angeles to Sydney.

Page 61

93. a. When an integer is divided by 2, the only possible remainders are 0 and 1. A remainder of 0 shows that 2 is a factor of the number, and a remainder of 1 shows that 2 is not a factor of the number. Given four consecutive integers, the remainders when divided by 2 have to be one of these two sequences: 0, 1, 0, 1; or 1, 0, 1, 0. In either case, exactly two of the four integers have 2 as a factor.

   b. When an integer is divided by 3, the only possible remainders are 0, 1, and 2, so with four consecutive integers, the remainders must be one of these sequences: 0, 1, 2, 0; 1, 2, 0, 1; or 2, 0, 1, 2. In each case, the remainder of 0 appears at least once in the sequence, showing that at least one of the four numbers is divisible by 3.

   c. This answer is given twice—as a mathematical proof and as a proof a student might think of.

   Mathematical proof:

   For any divisor n, there are n possible remainders: 0, 1, 2, ..., $n - 1$. The remainders are consecutive for consecutive dividends, and once the nth remainder ($n - 1$) is reached, the next remainder starts the cycle again (at 0). Thus, for a divisor of n, any n consecutive integers used as dividends will have n different remainders and thus will contain only one integer that is divisible by n. Applying this general principle to the specific case of four consecutive integers, we see that any divisor of 4 or more has four or more possible remainders and, since these remainders run consecutively, at most one of the four consecutive integers will have a remainder of 0 for that divisor. This shows that no two of the four consecutive integers can have a factor higher than 3.

   Student's proof:

   When you divide by 4, the remainder has to be 0, 1, 2, or 3, and when you divide consecutive integers by 4, the remainders are consecutive. There are four remainders and only four consecutive numbers to divide by 4, so no remainder will be repeated. This shows that 4 can't be a factor of more than one of the four consecutive integers. Analogous reasoning can be used for any number higher than 4.

> Because it looked more like a hippopotamus than any of the other animals that had walked by did. (Actually, the word is from two Greek words meaning roughly "river horse," presumably because hippopotamuses are so often found lolling in the water.)

If some of the students can work with negative numbers and think they have found a counterexample to parts **a** and **b** by listing, say -1, 0, 1, and 2, you may have to remind them that (by definition of "factor") every integer except 0 is a factor of 0. The proofs below assume the four integers are positive, but analogous arguments would apply if they were negative or if they were a mixture of negative, zero, and positive.

Page 62

94. Add three and a half to the product of one and two fifths and three and one fourth. What is the answer?

$[1\frac{2}{5} \times 3\frac{1}{4} + 3\frac{1}{2} = 7/5 \times 13/4 + 7/2 = 91/20$
$+ 7/2 = (91 + 70)/20 = 161/20 = 8 \ 1/20]$

Pages 63–80, 91–93

One of the most important mathematical tools is the ability to recognize and use analogies. When we show our students how to solve a few problems, we want them to apply analogous reasoning to other problems. When we introduce new material, we want them to recognize the similarities and respect the differences between these new ideas and what they already know.

Analogues abound in mathematics. As examples: Multiplication and addition are analogous, as are division and subtraction. Telling the time seventeen hours after twelve o'clock (using a twelve-hour clock) is analogous to finding the least residue of 17 (mod 12). Arithmetic operations in base ten are analogous to those in base sixteen. A problem asking how many nickels are in $5.25 is analogous to one asking how much would have to be invested at 5% in order to earn $5.25 interest. Problems involving percents are readily translatable to problems involving fractions or decimals. And if you'll excuse the pun, the reasoning needed to prove plane geometry theorems often runs parallel to that needed for proving theorems in analytic geometry.

If we are to have students who easily recognize analogous situations in mathematics, it is necessary that they learn to look for similarities and differences, that they learn that order matters, that they learn to distinguish between situations that are close enough to be analogous and situations that are not, and that they have practice in forming analogies.

This could be accomplished utilizing only mathematical notions, but it is much easier for the students to learn when the practice exercises use everyday words not taken exclusively from any one subject area. (Presenting an assortment of topics also has the advantage of showing that analogies can be applied in numerous contexts.) Consequently, most of the material on the next few pages

has little to do with mathematics per se, but it has a great deal to do with building knowledge necessar to success in mathematics.

After the word "analogous" is introduced in the textbook, it will be assumed throughout the rest of the book that the students will understand an instruction such as, "Use analogous reasoning to show…."

Page 63

95. geometric figures

96. curt

97. old makes of cars

98. branches of mathematics

99. strange

100. kinds of triangles

Encourage alternate answers to these problems. We want the students to learn to notice various similarities among apparently different things, for such discernment is a prerequisite to the successfu use of analogical reasoning in mathematics.

Page 64

Other answers are not only possible but likely. Encourage class discussion of answers.

101. names of parts of arithmetic problems; produc (an answer, rather than part of the problem)

102. European capitals; Taipei

103. "new world" countries; Spain. (Some of the students may choose Canada as the exceptio to Spanish-language countries. This is a good opportunity for them to learn that Brazil's language is Portuguese, not Spanish.)

104. words on road signs; red light

105. foods grown on vines; fig

106. multiples of 3; 2

Page 65

Other answers are possible.

107. laboratory

108. bowling

109. 2

110. 2 feet

111. 1/8

Pages 66–69

112. lightning, thunder

113. original, copy

114. compliment, criticize

115. hope, dread

116. retrospect, hindsight

117. major, minor

118. recreation, hobby / time, distance / indicate, deduce / invention, imitation / universe, galaxy / tetrahedron, sphere

119. animal, plant / gridiron, diamond / pool, pot / human, animal / pot, gridiron / diamond, shale / plant, house

Pages 70–71

120. Hot is to cold as volcano is to glacier.

121. Elephant is to ant as vertebrate is to invertebrate.

122. Radar is to sonar as air is to water.

123. Acute is to obtuse as perceptive is to insensitive.

124. Hammer is to saw as batter is to slice. (I'm open to argument about "force, persuasion" being an acceptable choice.)

125. Challenge [Other answers are possible.] Crucial is to important as picayune is to trivial. Durable is to permanent as ephemeral is to transitory.

Many standardized tests measure knowledge by including analogies among the test questions. However, a wrong answer there may not indicate lack of knowledge about the subject matter. Instead, it may show confusion about what is being asked. This is because in everyday life we don't necessarily compare or contrast two pairs of things by using the standard analogical words "is to" and "as," and these words don't make a lot of sense in such a context unless either we think about them and figure out how they're being used, or we've seen them used previously in such a way and now understand how they relate the terms to each other.

As you discuss this section with your class, keep in mind that an analogy using "is to" and "as" will not, to many of the students, immediately make

sense. To help them understand, choose a simple analogy and try stating it in various ways.

Ignoring whether or not good English is used, or even whether or not the statements are entirely accurate, here are some examples of other ways to state the analogy, "Up is to down as high is to low":

- Up and down are related in the same way that high and low are related.

- Up is related to down the way high is related to low.

- Up and down contrast in the way that high and low contrast.

- Up is different from down in the way that high is different from low.

- The relation between up and down is like the relation between high and low.

Similar examples can be formulated using such terms as these: dissimilar; opposite; opposed (to); reversed (from); contrary (to).

So that the students don't get the idea that the first two terms of an analogy must name opposites, you will probably want to show that analogies can be formed for other relationships, too. At the same time you give a nonstandard form, be sure also to state the standard form. For example,

- A cow and its calf are related in the way that a mare and its foal are related. (A cow is to its calf as a mare is to its foal.)

- Laugh and happy sound go together just like cry and sad sound go together. (Laugh is to happy sound as cry is to sad sound.)

- Green light means "go" just as red light means "stop." (Green light is to "go" as red light is to "stop.")

- Penthouse apartment is related to plenty of money in the same way that tenement flat is related to lack of money. (Penthouse apartment is to plenty of money as tenement flat is to lack of money.)

Stress two things: (1) an analogy must always make good sense; (2) an analogy cannot necessarily be formed from two pairs of terms even if the terms of one pair are related not only to each other but to the terms of the other pair. For example, a hammer and a wrench are both tools, and both are owned by humans; a dog and a cat are both pets, and both are owned by humans. Despite these similarities, however, it wouldn't make good sense to say any of these (or any of the 20 other statements that could be made from arranging the four terms in different orders):

Hammer is to wrench as dog is to cat.
Hammer is to wrench as cat is to dog.
Hammer is to dog as wrench is to cat.
Hammer is to cat as wrench is to dog.

Ask the students to think of analogies themselves (using "is to" and "as"), and let the class discuss whether or not the analogies created are good ones. This not only will supply examples on the students' level but will also lessen confusion about the meaning of an analogy stated in standard form.

Pages 72–73

To avoid having to list eight answers for each problem, a general solution is given here, and then only a first answer is given for each problem.

General rule:	term	is to	term
as	term	is to	term
If	first		second
	third		fourth
then	first		third
	second		fourth
and	second		first
	fourth		third
and	second		fourth
	first		third
and	third		first
	fourth		second
and	third		fourth
	first		second
and	fourth		second
	third		first
and	fourth		third
	second		first

126. typhoon Philippines hurricane West Indies

127. compliment flattery honesty exaggeration

128. complement complete supplement enhance

129. earthquake land tidal wave sea

130. theorem conjecture proof guesswork

In the "don't be fooled" paragraph on page 72, the second sentence is accurate only if the four given terms are different from each other. If two of

the terms are the same, there will be only twelve distinct ways to arrange them, of which just four will be in correct order for forming analogies. For example, given the terms

ocean, lake, lake, puddle

they can be arranged as

ocean, lake, lake, puddle
ocean, lake, puddle, lake
ocean, puddle, lake, lake
lake, ocean, lake, puddle
lake, ocean, puddle, lake
lake, lake, ocean, puddle
lake, lake, puddle, ocean
lake, puddle, ocean, lake
lake, puddle, lake, ocean
puddle, ocean, lake, lake
puddle, lake, ocean, lake
puddle, lake, lake, ocean

The only acceptable analogies would be

Ocean is to lake as lake is to puddle.
Lake is to ocean as puddle is to lake.
Lake is to puddle as ocean is to lake.
Puddle is to lake as lake is to ocean.

Pages 74–76

These problems will be too obscure for some of the students to figure out by themselves, and yet to invite a full class discussion could easily lead to so many suggestions and comments that confusion, rather than solution, results. Instead, break up the class into several small groups, say three to five students each, and let each group work independently on solving the problem.

Page 74

131. [(sightless) (seashore)]er = [(no see) (seacoast)]er = [no sea seacoast]er = [coast]er = coaster

(Edinburgh girl) that starts in (the right direction) = lass that starts in (the direction for "right") = lass that starts in gee = lass that starts in g = glass (set) (tahhsittocS) = place (backward Scottish hat) = place (backward tam) = <u>place mat</u>

(recordless) (attempt without reason) = (recordless) (try without why) = (recordless) (try without y) = (record less) tr = platter – tr = <u>plate</u>

Result: Coaster is to glass as place mat is to plate.

The hint given won't be of much help to most students, but it might make sense to some living in rural areas. Although "gee" and "haw," the directions for "right" and "left," aren't often heard today, they were commonly used for directing horses and mules before tractors and automobiles took over.

Page 75

132. slight = disdainful disregard = <u>cut</u>

(atmosphere) following (_{case} symbolic hydrogen) = air following (lower case H) = <u>hair</u>

doss before a cheer = dossyay = dossier = <u>file</u>

(more than one) {hefty [(short Bradley) (without a backer)]} = plural of {hefty [Brad uncapitalized]} = plural of {hefty brad} = hefty brads = <u>nails</u>

Result: Cut is to hair as file is to nails.

For the hint given in the students' text, the sweeping tool is a broom. The "ing" on the end gives us "brooming." We get "grooming" when we turn the first letter upside side and add a loop toward the left on the end of it, so the problem has something to do with grooming.

Page 76

133. (retrogressive bus) runs into {[used (knocking down knocking down knocking down knocking down)] but sightless} = (bus going backward) runs into {[used (flooring flooring flooring flooring)] but sightless} = sub runs into {[used (four flooring)] but sightless} = sub runs into {[used for flooring] but no eye} = sub runs into {tile but no i} = sub runs into tle = <u>subtle</u>

(cockney he) (unfettered) if = e (loose) if = <u>elusive</u>

(able able) (10 10 do) = (able two) (past 10's do) = (able to) (past tense do) = can did = <u>candid</u>

(10 10 victory) (tdividingo) a [(gnu) (do do)] = (past 10's victory) (dividing in to) a [(new) (two do)] = (past tense win) (dividing in two) a [young (to-do)] = (won) (halving) a [young stir] = one having a youngster = a parent = <u>apparent</u>

Result: Subtle is to elusive as candid is to apparent.

In the WARNING paragraph in the students' text, the last sentence has nothing to do with the hint. The hint was contained in the words "delicate," "difficult to grasp," "forthright," and "obvious," which are approximate synonyms for the terms of the analogy.

Pages 77–80

134. As it stands, the analogy is a poor one, because the similarities are not enough to support the conclusion. That is, there are too many potential important differences unaccounted for: Does one house use insulated storm windows and the other house not? Does one furnace burn gas with 90% efficiency and the other with only 60% efficiency? Is one thermostat set at 72°F and the other at 68°F? Are outside doors of one house opened more often than outside doors of the other house (maybe because of children or pets)? Are the basement heat registers kept open in one house but not in the other?

We are reasoning by analogy any time we use a previous experience to predict the outcome of a new experience. For example, "That plant had green leaves and I was told to pull it out because it was a weed. This plant has green leaves, so it must be a weed, too." Or, "I got yelled at yesterday because I was running in the school hallway. If I run in the school hallway today, I'll get yelled at today, too."

Make sure the students understand that when reasoning by analogy assumes a cause-and-effect relationship, it is the quality of the relationship that determines whether or not the analogy is a good one. In the first example above, the speaker assumes that having green leaves causes a plant to be classified as a weed. Since having green leaves has no bearing on whether or not a plant is called a weed, the analogy is a poor one. In the second example above, it is assumed that running in the school hallway causes the runner to be repri-

199

manded. On the surface, this assumption is false, and yet the analogy is a good one because running in the hallway can be dangerous and it is this potential danger, rather than the running itself, that results in the reprimand.

The students will automatically look for similarities between analogous situations, but you may have to lead them to evaluate the relative importance of the points of agreement.

All analogous situations have differences, too, and some students are likely to say that a particular analogy is poor because differences outnumber similarities. Consequently, you may have to stress to the students that when they are deciding on the quality of an analogy, they are to distinguish between important and unimportant differences.

Here are some other examples of reasoning by analogy.

> That steel bar is metal, and my fingernail doesn't make a dent in it. Since this aluminum foil is also metal, my fingernail won't make a dent in it, either. (Poor.)

> My house is at sea level, and I got scalded when some boiling water splashed on my wrist. I'm now near a campfire on top of a mountain 15,000 feet high, and my wrist will get scalded if boiling water splashes on it. (Poor, since water boils at a much lower temperature at high altitudes outdoors.)

> My friend went to a beauty parlor for a facial, and when they were done she didn't have any wrinkles. So if I go to that beauty parlor and have the same operator give me a facial, then I won't have any wrinkles. (Not enough information. How old is my friend? How old am I? Did my friend have any wrinkles before the treatment? Do I have any wrinkles?)

> Three different batteries for my toy lasted only a month each. So if I get another of the same kind of battery and use the toy the same amount of time, the new battery will last only a month. (Good.)

Use class discussion for these problems. We want the students to be exposed to the reasoning of their classmates and to hear the arguments they use.

Page 79

135. This is a poor analogy. Word-processing programs vary greatly in ease of application, quality of training manuals, and quality of user support given by the manufacturer. Also, different brands of computers may have different internal operating systems. Because a program for, say an MS-DOS computer, can't be read by an Apple computer, two different programs must be created, and the result is that sometimes the program for one operating system is much easier to work with than the program for the other system.

Make sure the students recognize Moira's analogy: I've tried and my family have tried to use our word-processing program, and we have all found it to be an unpleasant experience. Therefore, if my job should require me to use a word-processing program, I would find using it an unpleasant experience and would not enjoy my job.

Notice that Moira's reasoning takes a particular case and draws from it a general conclusion. That is, she has found that using a particular word-processing program on a particular computer has been a disagreeable experience, and she concludes that using any word-processing program on any computer will be a disagreeable experience.

Page 80

136. This is a good analogy. If you're going to do your own barking (if Mr. Smith is going to make all the decisions), then you're going to stay on watch yourself (then he is doing his executives jobs) and so you don't need a watchdog (and so he doesn't need executives).

Ask the students to state the analogy being drawn: Having an executive but making all decisions yourself is like having a watchdog and doing your own barking.

Page 81

137. Put two balls in each pan. The scales either (1) balance or (2) don't balance.

Suppose (1). Remove three of the four balls weighed and put one of the two unweighed balls in the empty pan. If the scales balance, the odd ball is the sixth ball. If they don't balance, the odd ball is the one that was added.

Suppose (2). Then the odd ball is one of the four weighed. Remove the two balls from one of the pans and lay them aside. Transfer a ball from the other pan to the empty pan. Either the scales now (3) balance or (4) don't balance.

Suppose (3). Then the odd ball is one of the two removed. See "Final Weighing" below.

Suppose (4). Then the odd ball is one of the two not removed. See "Final Weighing" below.

<u>Final Weighing</u>: The odd ball is known to be one of two particular balls. Put one of these in one pan, and put one of the other four balls (known to be of normal weight) in the other pan. If the scale balances, the odd ball is the one (of the two suspects) not weighed this time. If the scale doesn't balance, the odd ball is the one (of the two suspects) weighed this time.

Page 82

138. You invest two thousand dollars. Half is at five percent and half is at six percent. How much annual interest is earned? [5% of $1000 + 6% of $1000 = $110]

Once the students have decoded the puzzle, you may have to remind them that an interest rate is understood to be an annual rate unless otherwise indicated.

Page 83

139. Not given. Let the students battle it out.

This is strictly a class discussion problem. If you think, as I did, that this problem's answer is so obvious that your students will be insulted by being given the problem, you have a surprise coming. I've found that the usual answers are gains of 0, $10, $20, or $30, with an occasional answer of a loss of $10, $20, or $30.

Ask the students to call out their answers, and write all the answers on the chalkboard. Then ask, "Who wants to start? Tell us which answer you got, and tell us how you got it." The hard part for the students comes when you say, after hearing the explanation, "We have some other answers here, and we can't have more than one right answer to the problem, so if you think another answer is right,

you should be able to tell us what's wrong with the reasoning we've just heard."

The time needed for the discussion usually takes at least a full class period. I've never told my students the answer to the problem. Instead, they have always managed to prove which answer is correct.

Page 84

This is another Diophantine problem.

140. They should buy 85 pounds of chicken ($51), 12 pounds of rolled roast ($40), and 3 pounds of pollock ($9).

Pages 85–90

141.

	Jane Doe
c.	IAMSOBRILLIANTTHAT
d.	IAMSOBRIMEIANEMHAT
e.	MSOBRIMEIANEMH
f.	MSOBRIMESISANEMSH
g.	BSOMIMESISAREMSH
h.	BSOMEIMESISAREMSHE
i.	SOMEIMESISAREMSELF
j.	SOMETIMESISCAREMYSELF

142. a. Three. When you pull out the first sock, its color doesn't matter. If the second sock is the same color, you're done. If it isn't, then you have one sock of each color, and the third sock has to be the same color as one of them.

b. Four. The reasoning is analogous to the reasoning for part **a**.

c. Five. Same kind of reasoning again.

d. $n + 1$. Same kind of reasoning again.

Ask the students how their answers would change if the drawer had (1) less than 10 of each color or (2) more than 10 of each color.

143. 21 seconds. The first ring starts at 0 time, the second 5 seconds later, and so on, up to the fifth, which starts 20 seconds after the start of the first. Counting 1 second to wait for the end of the fifth ring, that totals 21 seconds.

144. 12 weeks. The idea here is to find the least common multiple (LCM) of 4 days and 3 weeks—i.e., 4 days and 21 days—and that is 84 days, or 12 weeks.

Notice that the LCM, 12, was the product of the given number of days, 4, and the given number of weeks, 3. That makes sense, for to get our answer of 12 weeks, we took $[4 \times (3 \times 7)]/7 = (4 \times 3) \times (7/7) = 4 \times 3$. Point this out to the students and ask if we can always take this kind of shortcut for such a problem. (The answer is no. It always gives us an answer of when the event will occur again, but it tells us the *next* time the event will occur again only when the two numbers of days are mutually prime. In the problem given, the numbers of days, 4 and 21, were mutually prime. If the times between events were 4 days and 2 weeks, for example, the next occurrence would be in 4 weeks, not 8 weeks. This is because the LCM of 4 days and 2 weeks, or 4 days and 14 days, is 28 days, not 56 days.)

145. If the first native told the truth, then the second native lied. If the first native lied, then the second native told the truth. Either way, one of them told the truth and the other lied, so the third native had to be lying.

146. a–b. Whether or not the first native is a liar, he would claim that he is not a liar. Then the first part of the second native's statement brands the second native as a liar, and the second part of his statement (since we now know he was lying) makes the first native a truth-teller.

147. We're given that all roads lead either to a village or the jungle. There are no half-truths or half-lies, so the third native cannot be a liar (because if he were, then at least half of his statement would necessarily be true, a contradiction). This makes the first two natives liars.

148. Without other complications, the question could be, "If I were to ask you which branch of the road leads to the village, what would you say?" Consider the implications of the phrase, "If I were to ask." A liar would lie if asked directly, "Which branch leads to the village?" but will also lie about what he would answer **if** he were to be asked such a question. The result is that his answer will be the truth about

which branch leads to the village. The truth-teller would tell the truth in both cases.

A nice complication occurs, however, if we grant the liar the right to try to circumvent the stranger's deviousness by lying about the spirit, rather than the phrasing, of the question. You might like to invite the students to discuss this point and see if they can find a way aroun it, remembering that the stranger doesn't know whether he's asking the question of a truth-teller or a liar.

Pages 91–108

The students may not realize at first that they have worked with proportions many times before, and it would be helpful to remind them that every time the have added or subtracted fractions with unlike denominators they have written at least one propor-tion. For example, given the fractions 2/3 and 5/6 to add, they have written "2/3 = 4/6" and probably also "5/6 = 5/6."

It is important that the students have clear ideas about the parts of a proportion, their relation to each other, the significance of the equals sign, and the difference between a ratio and a proportion.

"Equals" is a symmetric relation, so this is always true:

If item 1 = item 2, then item 2 = item 1.

All fractions are ratios. Although there are vari-ous kinds of ratios, all ratios in this book are frac-tions, so for the most part the two words can be used synonymously by the students.

There is a difference in the thinking involved about the two concepts, however: a fraction, say 3/4, is thought of as 3 parts out of every 4 parts (of something), whereas the ratio 3/4 is thought of as "3 to 4" because a ratio compares the two things.

For example, in a household com-prised of a baby, two parents, and a grandparent, 3 out of 4, or 3/4, of the people are adults, and the ratio of adults to total people is 3 to 4, or 3/4.

A ratio has two terms:

$$\frac{\text{first term}}{\text{second term}}, \text{ or } \frac{\text{numerator}}{\text{denominator}}.$$

A proportion has two sides, left-hand side = right-hand side, or first ratio = second ratio, and four terms:

$$\frac{\text{first term}}{\text{second term}} = \frac{\text{third term}}{\text{fourth term}}.$$

A proportion is read as: first term is to second term as third term is to fourth term.

As defined here, a proportion consists of two ratios separated by an equals sign, so for our purposes neither of the following is a proportion:

- 4/2 = 2 [but 4/2 = 2/1 is a proportion]
- 4/2 = 24/3 – 6 [but 4/2 = (24 – 18)/3 is a proportion, as is 4/2 = 24/(3 + 9)]

In common usage, the terms "ratio" and "proportion" are sometimes used interchangeably. In mathematics, however, the two terms are *never* synonymous. Here are some of the differences:

- A proportion is a statement of equality; a ratio is not.
- A proportion contains an equals sign; a ratio does not.
- A ratio gives the relative sizes of two things; a proportion is a statement that two *pairs* of things have the same relative sizes.
- A ratio is not in itself a statement; a proportion is.
- A proportion has four terms; a ratio has only two.
- A proportion is an equation; a ratio is not.

Pages 91–93

All of the proportions are listed here, although the students are required to state only three of them. However, only the first of the analogies is shown here. In particular, notice that we consider the proportion a/b = c/d to be distinct from the proportion c/d = a/b, even though they are equivalent statements.

149. Yes. 2/6 = 5/15; 2 is to 6 as 5 is to 15; 2/5 = 6/15; 6/2 = 15/5; 6/15 = 2/5; 5/15 = 2/6; 5/2 = 15/6; 15/5 = 6/2; 15/6 = 5/2.

150. No.

151. Yes. 8/16 = 6/12; 8 is to 16 as 6 is to 12; 8/6 = 16/12; 16/8 = 12/6; 16/12 = 8/6; 6/12 = 8/16; 6/8 = 12/16; 12/6 = 16/8; 12/16 = 6/8.

152. Yes. 8/48 = 6/36; 8 is to 48 as 6 is to 36; 8/6 = 48/36; 48/8 = 36/6; 48/36 = 8/6; 6/36 = 8/48; 6/8 = 36/48; 36/6 = 48/8; 36/48 = 6/8.

153. No.

154. Yes. (1/2)/(2/3) = 6/8; l/2 is to 2/3 as 6 is to 8; (1/2)/6 = (2/3)/8; (2/3)/(1/2) = 8/6; (2/3)/8 = (1/2)/6; 6/8 = (1/2)/(2/3); 6/(1/2) = 8/(2/3); 8/6 = (2/3)/(1/2); 8/(2/3) = 6/(1/2).

If the students don't believe this, ask them to simplify the left-hand side of the first equation: (1/2)/(2/3) = (1/2) × (3/2) = 3/4 = 6/8.

It is not suggested that you raise the matter yourself, but some of the students may conjecture, since any proportion can be written as an analogy, that any numeric analogy can be written as a proportion. If they do bring it up, encourage them to explore the idea. They should be able to think of various counterexamples to the conjecture. For instance, if we're talking about differences between numbers, then

1 is to 2 as 5 is to 6, but 1/2 ≠ 5/6.

Or if we're talking about multiplying a number by itself, then

9 is to 3 as 25 is to 5, but 9/3 ≠ 25/5.

In each of these cases, however, no pair of numbers was a ratio, for a ratio, by definition, is a fraction—i.e., an indicated *quotient* of two numbers—and this should be made clear to the students. In the first case above, for instance, to talk about the *difference* between 1 and 2 and then to write "1/2" is contradictory. Although nonproportional numeric analogies can be formed, nonproportional numeric analogies cannot be formed when the numbers compared are ratios.

Pages 94–108

The problems are arranged in their approximate order of difficulty, and problems already done can be used for reference in a current proof. When a problem is easier than a preceding one, it is probably because the easier problem uses as part of its proof the statement proved by the harder problem.

Although they look innocuous enough, these problems require critical thinking and will result in a decidedly improved understanding of ratios and proportions.

Keep in mind that to find the answer to such a problem is one thing, but to prove it, particularly without the help of algebra, is considerably more difficult. (If your students have studied algebra, encourage them to use that knowledge for these proofs.)

The students may need frequent reminders to

choose numbers of their own so that they can see how a problem works. Encourage them to start each problem with easy numbers. For example, if a problem says that two terms of the proportion are the same, they could start with 1/2 = 2/4 or 2/4 = 4/8; or if the terms are all distinct, they could start with 1/2 = 3/6 or 2/4 = 3/6. Once they see how the problem works for these numbers, they can try to generalize their findings so that specific numbers don't have to be used. This generalization is, of course, the hard part of the problem and requires a different level of critical thinking (and a different side of the brain) than merely understanding the problem and trying it out with specific numbers.

Use class discussion to help your students graduate from an intuitive understanding to the formulation of a proof that their intuition is correct. It will be helpful if you will

- remind them that if both numerator and denominator of a fraction are multiplied or divided by the same (nonzero) number, the fraction's value doesn't change. (Mention again that they've done such multiplication and division when adding or subtracting fractions with unlike denominators.)

- remind them that dividing a fraction by a number is the same as multiplying the fraction by the number's reciprocal.

- teach them that both sides of an equation can be multiplied or divided by the same (nonzero) number, or the same number can be added to both sides or subtracted from both sides, and the result will also be an equation.

- Show them several examples and assign a few problems for practice, possibly along these lines:

  1) Change each fraction into a fraction having a denominator of 12: 1/2, 2/3, 5/6

  2) Find a common denominator for each pair of fractions, and express both as fractions having that denominator: 2/3, 3/4; 1/2, 3/7; 2/5, 3/20

     [Notice that the least common denominator (LCD) is not asked for. Encourage the students to realize that a pair of fractions can have an infinite number of common denominators.]

  3) Find the LCD for each pair of fractions,

and express both as fractions having the denominator: 6/12, 6/8; 6/16, 2/4; 8/24, 4/6

  4) Reduce each fraction as far as possible: 4/6, 10/20, 15/25

  5) Multiply both terms by 2, 3, and 5: 1/2, 3 5, 2/6

  6) Multiply both sides by 3: 1/2 = 3/6; 8/5 = 16/10

  7) Divide both sides by 2: 2/1 = 6/3; 8/9 = 24/27

Even when they can prove something *orally*, you should not expect students pursuing a general curriculum to be able to prove it in *writing*, at least not with a conventional proof. Instead, you might like to suggest they use diagrams (with numbered or lettered parts, if they wish) and arrows to go along with a written explanation.

You will notice that on some pages a list of selected problems proved so far is included. This helps the students remember some properties of proportions and serves as a handy reference if needed for the current problem. It is also a sneaky way to let the students know that not everything included on a page is needed for the problem they're doing.

Page 95

155. a. Multiply both sides of the proportion by the product of the denominators. Divide both sides by a numerator. Reduce as far as possible. The result says the denominators are equal.

    b. Multiply both sides by a denominator and reduce as far as possible. The result says the numerators are equal.

    c. Division by zero is not defined, so we can never divide by zero.

The theorem of parts **a–b** will be used in later proofs, so it would be a good idea to make sure the students understand it and can say it. The correct statement of the theorem includes the stipulation that the numerators are nonzero. This was omitted here because a condition stated for this series of problems excluded zero as any term of a proportion used here.

For part **c**, most students know they are not allowed to divide by zero, but they seldom understand why. It might help to point out that division is defined in terms of multiplication and so any division answer has to be verifiable by multiplication. (For example, 12/3 = 4, because $4 \times 3 = 12$.) Therefore, if there is any "division" problem that is not verifiable by multiplication, then that kind of division is not defined. This is the case for division by 0, because for 12/0 = ?, whatever we replace ? with will give us $? \times 0 = 0$, not $? \times 0 = 12$. So the reason that division by zero is not allowed is because it is not defined. Read on, however.

For 0/0, we have a different situation. Here, any answer we get is verifiable by multiplication. For example, 0/0 = 4, since $4 \times 0 = 0$; and $0/0 = 87\frac{1}{2}$, because $87\frac{1}{2} \times 0 = 0$. The problem, however, is that all arithmetic operations are defined to have unique answers, but 0/0 has an infinite number of answers rather than a unique one. We see that for this case, too, division by 0 is not defined.

Page 96

156. Use the product of the denominators as a common denominator, and convert the two ratios to ratios having this denominator. The denominators are now equal, so the numerators are equal (problem 155) and the problem is proved. (The left-hand numerator is the product of the extremes, and the right-hand numerator is the product of the means.)

Page 97

157. Suppose the second ratio's terms are equal. Then that ratio is worth 1. But the first ratio isn't worth 1 (because its terms are unequal), and so the two ratios aren't equal and therefore aren't proportional. This contradicts what we're given, which means our supposition has to be wrong, and so the second ratio's terms have to be unequal.

The power of the indirect proof lies both in its simplicity of concept and in its ability to prove statements for which a convenient direct proof cannot be found. The example in the students' text does not represent the kind of problem for which an indirect proof is most effective, for the problem there can be more easily proved with a direct proof. (Direct proof: By definition of a proportion, both ratios must be equal. Since one ratio has a value of 1, the other ratio must also have a value of 1.) However, the

example does illustrate simply and clearly how an indirect proof works. Here is another simple example you might like to use with your class.

EXAMPLE
Problem: Prove that 12/3 $\neq$ 6.

> (Indirect) Proof: Suppose 12/3 = 6. Then (because division is defined as the inverse of multiplication) $6 \times 3 = 12$. But $6 \times 3 \neq 12$ (because $6 \times 3 = 18$, and by definition a multiplication answer is unique), so we have a contradiction. Therefore, our supposition must be wrong, and so 12/3 $\neq$ 6.

Ask the class, "What if no contradiction is found? Does that prove the supposition true?" (The answer is no. Maybe we're just not bright enough to find the contradiction.)

A contradiction isn't always inevitable, for a statement assumed to be true may not necessarily be true at all. One of the most notable examples of this was discovered early in the 18th century when Girolamo Saccheri, an Italian Jesuit priest, set out to vindicate Euclid.

A popular belief at that time said that the postulate, "Through a given point not on a line, exactly one line is parallel to the given line," was redundant, that it could be proved from Euclid's other postulates and, consequently, that Euclid had erred in postulating it. Attempts to prove this succeeded only when other postulates were used instead, so for these proofs Euclid's postulate might as well have been used in the first place.

The controversy went on—was the postulate necessary, or wasn't it? Saccheri, an extremely able logician who was convinced that it was indeed necessary, decided to use an indirect proof. He denied the postulate with the idea that the resulting geometry would have to be self-contradictory, but despite his excellent efforts, no contradiction evolved, and his treatise on his findings became, in fact, a foundation for non-Euclidean geometry.

Apparently, however, the implications of Saccheri's treatise weren't fully considered, for it wasn't until the next century that Lobachevky (1826) and Bolyai (1832) developed hyperbolic geometry (by postulating two lines instead of one line parallel to a given line) and Riemann (1854) developed elliptic geometry (by postulating no lines parallel to a given line).

Page 98

158. We're given an equation having (a product of) two numbers on each side. Choose a number from the left-hand side, and divide both sides of the equation by this number. Reduce the left-hand side so that this number is eliminated. Do the same thing for a number from the right-hand side (choose, divide, reduce). The result is a proportion in which the given left-hand pair are the extremes, and the given right-hand pair are the means.

   a. It doesn't matter which pair is chosen to be the extremes because equality is symmetric. That is, the proof above used the left-hand pair as the extremes, but we could have switched the sides of the equation so that the right-hand side became the left-hand side, and the proof would then have used the other pair as the extremes.

   b–c. This is implicit in the proof, which said only to choose a number and didn't specify which one.

   d. This is implicit in the statements of **a** and **b**.

Don't let your students reason that this problem can be proved by using problem 156 as evidence, for problem 156 is the converse of this one, and converses are not always true. For example: if something is a cat, then it is an animal; but it is not true that if something is an animal, then it is a cat.

   This is an easy problem, once the students start thinking seriously about how to apply the hint given, and it is suggested that you don't give any hints about how to apply the hint. However, you might like to give them several examples (similar to the one in their text) to make sure they understand what the problem is claiming.

Pages 99–100

159. Use problem 156 to get the product of one pair of numbers = the product of another pair of numbers. Then use problem 158 to arrange

   a. the means

   b. the extremes

   in the other order.

160. Use problem 156 to get product of extremes = product of means. Then, using problem 158,

choose the two numbers on the right-hand sid (the old means) to be the extremes of a new proportion. Choose the old second term as the new first term, and choose the old first term as the new second term.

Page 101

161. We take the given proportion and add 1 to bot sides (2nd/2nd on the left, 4th/4th on the right) and simplify:

$$\frac{1st}{2nd} = \frac{3rd}{4th}, \text{ so } \frac{1st}{2nd} + \frac{2nd}{2nd} = \frac{3rd}{4th} + \frac{4th}{4th}, \text{ and so}$$

$$\frac{1st + 2nd}{2nd} = \frac{3rd + 4th}{4th}, \text{ which is what we were to pro}$$

Although the way to prove this problem is glaringly obvious when algebra is used, I don't think it is at a obvious when numbers are used. Consequently, a hint was given. Even with the hint, not all students will think of expressing 1 in one way for the left-han side and in another way for the right-hand side.

   When the students have seen how to prove this problem, ask what would happen if we subtracted, instead of added, the denominators to the numerators. (You'll probably have to start with improper fractions unless your students are used to working with negative numbers.)

Pages 102–104

162. The students may come up with two answers for the two parts of the problem, but both answers can be the same: A proportion can be formed, so problem 156 guarantees that our four given numbers can be paired in such a way that the product of one pair = the product of the other pair. Choose any number for the first term of the proportion (problem 158). The (problem 158 again) the other number in that pair will be the fourth term, and the remaining two numbers will be the second and third term (in either order).

163. a. Yes. 4/6 = 10/15; three terms, but not the fourth, have 2 as a factor.

   b. Suppose a proportion is possible. Then it takes the form

      1st term/2nd term = 3rd term/4th term.

Multiply both sides by 2nd. Reduce the left-hand side, leaving only 1st, a whole number. Then the new right-hand side, too, must be a whole number, so 4th divides the product 2nd × 3rd. This is a contradiction, for 4th can't do this unless it is 1 or unless it has a factor in common with 2nd or 3rd, and we're given that neither of these is true. Therefore, the supposition has to be wrong, and so a proportion is not possible.

c. We will call the given common factor "factor."

1) We can write the proportion made from the new numbers as

1st term/2nd term = 3rd term/4th term.

Multiply both sides by 1 in the form of factor/factor. The resulting terms are the original numbers.

2) Given the equation 1st term/2nd term = 3rd term/4th term, we can reduce to lower terms the fraction on each side without changing the truth value of the equation. It follows, if we suppose that the original numbers can form a proportion, that the new numbers can form the same relative proportion stated in lower terms. However, this conclusion contradicts the condition given for this problem, so such a supposition would be wrong. Therefore, the original numbers cannot form a proportion.

164. Once the proportion is formed, the two ratios can be inverted (problem 160), so the first term could have been the second term. Equality is symmetric, so the first term could have been the third term, and the second term could have been the fourth term. This shows that the first term could have been in any of the four positions. But any of the four numbers can be chosen as the first term (problem 162), so it follows that any of the numbers can be chosen for any of the terms.

Page 105

165. See the proof of problem 162. In effect, these theorems are proved there:

1) If a proportion can be formed from four given numbers, then any one of the numbers can be used as the first term.

2) If a proportion can be formed from four given numbers, one of which has been chosen as a first term, then at least two of the three unchosen numbers can be used as the second term.

For this current problem, we'll use each theorem in its contrapositive form:

1) Given four numbers: if one of them cannot be used as the first term of a proportion, then the four numbers cannot be the terms of a proportion.

2) Given four numbers, of which one has been chosen to be the first term of a potential proportion: if at least two of the three unchosen numbers cannot be used as the second term, then no proportion can be formed from the four given numbers.

Statement (1) proves part **b**, and statement (2) proves part **a**.

For those students who think it's unfair to use as an authority something proved on the way to proving something else, when that "something proved" wasn't stated explicitly at the time, here is a proof (from scratch) of part **a** of the problem:

Suppose the problem's statement is false. Then all three of the remaining numbers must be tried as a second term before we can say for certain whether or not a proportion can be formed. If either of the first two (of the remaining three) numbers had worked, then we'd already know the answer. So neither of the first two numbers worked, and the supposition is that we could possibly get a proportion by using the last remaining number as a second term. But if this were true, then when we switched the proportion's means (permitted by problem 159) we'd get a proportion whose second term was one of the two numbers already rejected. This is a contradiction, so the supposition has to be wrong. Therefore, the problem's statement is true.

This can be proved from scratch, but it's easier to use the theorems implicit in the proof of problem

162. To do this, however, it is convenient to use the contrapositives of the theorems, so you may have some groundwork to do with your class.

Give the students several examples of times they have used the contrapositive of a statement, instinctively knowing that the contrapositive was true because the statement was true:

- A teacher tells the class they're going to have a test, and the minimum passing score is 70%. The message given is, "If you're going to pass, then your score must be at least 70%." The students automatically know that if their score is not at least 70%, then they aren't going to pass.

- A youngster is assigned nightly dishwashing, an unloved task. Upset when told (s)he is too young to go skating with a group of friends, (s)he says, "If I'm old enough to do the dishes, then I'm old enough to go skating." Rephrased, this says, "If I'm not too young for the dishes, then I'm not too young to go skating," which is the contrapositive of what the youngster would really like to say, "If I'm too young to go skating, then I'm too young to do the dishes."

- Janine says the local vet doesn't seem to like animals very much, and Ricardo, who can't believe there's a vet alive who doesn't like animals, answers, "If he didn't like animals, he wouldn't be a vet," the contrapositive of, "If he's a vet, then he likes animals," or, "All vets like animals."

Toss in other examples of the everyday use of contrapositives, as well, so that the students realize how often such statements are used:

- If Bennetti weren't brave, she wouldn't be an astronaut ≡ If Bennetti is an astronaut, then she's brave.

- Nobody I know says things like that ≡ If it's anyone I know, then (s)he doesn't say things like that.

- If you can't say something nice, then keep quiet ≡ If you can't keep quiet, then (at least) say something nice.

- If Jankowski weren't an outstanding athlete, then he wouldn't be in the Olympic games ≡ If Jankowski is in the Olympic games, then he's an outstanding athlete.

- All mannerly people are polite ≡ All impolite people are unmannerly.

Next, help the students realize that a false statement has a false contrapositive:

- If someone eats junk food, then that person is fat ≡ If someone isn't fat, then that person doesn't eat junk food.

- If you like a class a lot, then you get terrific grades in it ≡ If you don't get terrific grades in a class, then you don't like it a lot.

- If a man has blue eyes, then he is a blond ≡ If a man isn't a blond, then he doesn't have blue eyes.

At this point, the students should recognize the contrapositive of an "if-then" statement and believe that a statement and its contrapositive can be freely exchanged for one another. Now help them transfer and apply their knowledge to mathematics:

- If two ratios are equal, then they are proportional ≡ If two ratios are not proportional, then they are not equal.

- If a fraction can be reduced, then it is not in its lowest terms ≡ If a fraction is in its lowest terms, then it cannot be reduced.

- If two numbers are equal, then all of their factors are common to both of them ≡ If not all of the factors of two numbers are common to both numbers, then the numbers are not equal.

Finally, ask the class for other examples of mathematical "if-then" statements, and ask that the contrapositives also be stated.

The indirect proofs used for other problems in this series have, for the most part, been proofs of the contrapositives of the statements wanted. For part c(2) of problem 163, for example, it was proved that if the original numbers can form a proportion, then the new numbers, too, can form a proportion. This was the contrapositive of the problem to be proved: If the new numbers cannot form a proportion, then the original numbers cannot form a proportion, either.

Page 106

166. a. No. We've already tried and failed with 1st/2nd $\stackrel{?}{=}$ 3rd/4th and with 1st/2nd $\stackrel{?}{=}$ 4th/3rd. Switching 1st and 2nd would merely result

in inverting the would-be proportions already tried. Problem 160 guarantees that we can invert the ratios of a proportion, so if switching 1st and 2nd would give us a proportion, then inverting both ratios of this proportion would also give us a proportion, contradicting our first two failures.

b. 1) Yes; no. Given the numbers 1, 2, 3, and 6, if we choose 1 and 6 for the first two terms, we won't get a proportion, but that certainly isn't enough to show that $1/2 = 3/6$ isn't a proportion.

2) We quit trying because a proportion isn't possible; no. Problem 165 says we need try only two out of the three remaining numbers as the second term.

c. No. Problems 162 and 164 say that any number can be used as the first term, if a proportion is possible.

Page 107

Notice that an indirect proof is used here.

167. No. Suppose four consecutive numbers can be used to form a proportion. Any of the four can be chosen as the first term (problem 164), so choose the largest. If the smallest is the second term, then this ratio has to be larger (because the numbers are farther apart) than the other ratio, so the smallest number can't be the second term. The means can be switched in a proportion (problem 159), so if the smallest number could be the third term, then it could also be the second. We've already established that it can't be the second, so this means that it can't be the third, either, which leaves it to be the fourth term and leaves the middle two numbers to be the second and third terms in either order. We can switch the extremes of a proportion (problem 159), so our proportion can be written as

$$\frac{1st}{2nd} = \frac{3rd}{4th},$$

where 1st, 2nd, 3rd, and 4th are the four consecutive numbers in order. Use problem 156 to get

$$1st \times 4th = 2nd \times 3rd,$$

and divide both sides by 4th to get

$$1st = \frac{2nd \times 3rd}{4th}.$$

The left-hand side (1st) is a whole number, so the right-hand side, too, is a whole number, which means that every factor of 4th is also a factor of either 2nd or 3rd. Two consecutive numbers cannot have any common factors (other than 1), so all factors of 4th have to be factors of 2nd. But this is impossible, because 4th is larger than 2nd. Our supposition led to a contradiction, so the supposition has to be wrong. Therefore, four consecutive numbers cannot be used to form a proportion.

Page 108

168. The question to be answered is:

If we start with $\frac{1st}{2nd} = \frac{3rd}{4th}$, and end with $\frac{1st + 3rd}{2nd + 4th} \overset{?}{=} \frac{3rd}{4th}$, can the "?" be removed? The answer is yes and is proved by following these steps:

1) Apply problem 156 to the given proportion.

2) Add 3rd × 4th to both sides.

3) Apply the distributive principle to both sides, factoring out 4th on the left-hand side and 3rd on the right-hand side.

4) Apply problem 158 to get the desired result.

Here are the results after each step:

1) $1st \times 4th = 3rd \times 2nd$

2) $(1st \times 4th) + (3rd \times 4th) = (3rd \times 2nd) + (3rd \times 4th)$

3) $(1st + 3rd) \times 4th = 3rd \times (2nd + 4th)$

4) $\frac{1st + 3rd}{2nd + 4th} = \frac{3rd}{4th}$

This problem has been rated as one of the hardest in this series. First, the required manipulations are hard to visualize for a student who hasn't had algebra (and for some who have had algebra). Second, even after the students have overcome this difficulty, some of them will reach creative heights in their flights of fancy about what can legitimately be done to the parts of an equation.

The question posed by this problem is: If $a/b = c/d$, then does $(a + c)/(b + d) = c/d$? This is not at all the same thing as asking: If $a/b = c/d$, then does $(a/b) + (c/d) = c/d$? You are almost guaranteed that some of the students will use this incorrect version if you don't try to circumvent it, and you might like to discuss this with the class before assigning the problem.

The distributive property of multiplication over addition is used in the proof below, and the students may need reminding of this property and of the fact that equality is symmetric. That is, $a(b + c) = ab + ac$, so if we start with $a(b + c)$ we can get $ab + ac$, and if we start with $ab + ac$, we can get $a(b + c)$.

Page 109

169.　a.　4 days (8 jobs take 8×4 bricklayer-days = 32 bricklayer-days. We have 8 bricklayers, so we need 32 bricklayer-days ÷ 8 bricklayers = 4 days. Or more simply, we have 8 bricklayers and 8 jobs, 1 job per bricklayer. Since each job takes 4 days, we need 4 days.)

　　b.　16 (1 job per bricklayer every 4 days)

　　c.　4 (In 8 days, 1 bricklayer will do 2 jobs.)

　　d.　4 (10 jobs will take 40 bricklayer-days. We have 10 days, so we need 4 bricklayers.)

　　e.　6 (4 bricklayers each working 6 days = 24 bricklayer-days. Each job takes 4 of these, so 6 jobs can be done.)

The thing to realize about this problem is that each bricklayer works for four days to do one job. This is more easily seen if we think of a job in terms of bricklayer-days. We're given that 4 bricklayers each work for 4 days, which makes 16 bricklayer-days, to do 4 jobs. Then 16 bricklayer-days ÷ 4 jobs = 4 bricklayer-days per job. The problems become much simpler to do if we use this kind of rationale for them.

Page 110

170.　The first line shows the numbers of quarts the jugs hold. Successive lines show how many quarts are in each jug. Other solutions are possible.

12	9	4	
12	0	0	Start
3	9	0	
3	5	4	
7	5	0	
7	1	4	
11	1	0	
11	0	1	
2	9	1	
2	6	4	
6	6	0	

Page 111

171.　Each group of 200,001 people may all have different numbers of hairs (ranging from 0 through 200,000). The problem's statement is perhaps easier to see if we use an indirect proof. Suppose at most nine people have any given number of hairs. Then there are at most 200,001 × 9 people = 1,800,009 people. But New York City has a population of at least 1,800,010, so there are at least ten people there who have the same number of hairs on their heads.

My reference books didn't tell me the maximum number of hairs that can grow on a human head, s I pulled a figure out of the air.

Simplify the arithmetic involved by making the number of hairs range from 0 to 199,999 or from 1 to 200,000 before asking this question: Given a city of population 2,000,000, at least how many <u>pairs</u> o people have the same number of hairs on their heads?

This is a much tougher question than the one in the textbook. If the hairs on two heads match, that' one pair; if on three heads, that's three pairs; if on four heads, that's six pairs, and so on. Given h matching heads, the number of pairs is $h(h - 1)/2$.

Given two groups of 200,000 people, with all 200,000 in each group having different numbers of hairs, there are 200,000 pairs who match. Now consider the number of matching pairs if in the first group all have different numbers of hairs, and in th second group the first 199,999 have different numbers, but the 200,000th matches one of the others. Then this one also matches one of the ones in the first group. Out of our 400,000 people, we have fro the first group 1 who doesn't match anyone, 1 who matches 2 from the second group, and 199,998 wh match 199,998 from the second group. So the number of pairs we have = 199,998 + 3(3 − 1)/2 = 199,998 + 3 = 200,001. It is seen, then, that the number of matching pairs increases if, in any group of 200,000, two heads match. Now consider three groups of 200,000, with no matching heads in any one group. We now have each of the 200,000 matching two others, which means 3 pairs each, so that's 600,000 pairs of matching heads for the 600,000 people. For four such groups, the number of matching pairs would be $200,000 \times 4(4 - 1)/2 = 200,000 \times 6 = 1,200,000$ pairs for 800,000 people. In a population of 2,000,000, we could have ten such groups, and the number of matching pairs would be $200,000 \times 10(10 - 1)/2 = 200,000 \times 45 = 9,000,000$.

Page 112

This is another Diophantine problem.

172. They can buy 80 pounds of chicken ($48), 16 pounds of round steak ($40), and 4 pounds of pollock ($12).

This question was asked by Abraham Lincoln. When the person asked answered, "Five," Lincoln said, "No. A horse has only four legs. Calling a tail a leg doesn't make the tail a leg."

Page 113

173. a. yes

b. not enough information

174. a. not enough information

b. yes

c. yes

d. not enough information

These are relatively hard problems. They would be much easier if we had information about the numbers of problems on the two tests. As it stands, there may have been more problems on yesterday's test than today's, or vice versa, and we have to consider both possibilities in deciding on our answers.

Pages 114–123

175. You invested a thousand dollars at eight percent. Interest was compounded quarterly. How much did you have a year later? [1st quarter, 2% of $1000 = $20; 2nd quarter, 2% of $1020 = $20.40; 3rd quarter, 2% of $1040.40 = $20.81; 4th quarter, 2% of $1061.21 = $21.22; total = $1061.21 + $21.22 = $1082.43.]

176. We have a choice of either putting one or more weights in one pan and none in the other, or of putting weights in both pans in order to weigh the difference between the weights.

To weigh objects from 1 to 4 pounds, we put weights in the pans as follows: 1 = 1 and 0; 2 = 3 and 1; 3 = 3 and 0, 4 = 3 + 1 and 0.

The hard way to do the problem is to list the various combinations of weights to be used to weigh objects from 1 through 121 pounds. The easy way to do the problem is to notice that the weights are spaced so that each weight is one pound more than twice the sum of the previous weights.

To use the easy way, we do this: We go as far as we can with the lower weights, and then we subtract each number from the next higher weight, starting with the sum and going backwards to 0. That final weighing will give us only the next higher weight. Then we reverse the process, using that next higher weight and adding the previous weights from 1 through their sum.

For example, we already know how to weigh from 1 to 4 pounds. We take the next weight, 9 pounds, and subtract from it (by putting the previous weights in the other pan) 4, 3, 2, 1, and 0, to get weights of 5, 6, 7, 8, and 9 pounds. (To get a weight of 2 pounds, we had a weight in each pan, so to subtract 2 pounds from 9 pounds, we put the 9-pound weight in the pan with the lighter weight—i.e., 2 = 3 − 1, so 9 − 2 = 9 − 3 + 1 = (9 + 1) − 3. Similarly, to go beyond 9 pounds, we start with 9 and add the other combinations of 1, 2, 3, and 4 pounds to get totals of 10, 11, 12, and 13 pounds. We now see that our next weight, 27, can be combined with the previous weights to weigh anything from 27 − 13 = 14 pounds through 27 + 13 = 40 pounds. The same principle applies to the next weight, 81 pounds, allowing us to weigh anything from 81 − 40 = 41 pounds through 81 + 40 = 121 pounds.

The students should have discovered by now that 3, 9, 27, and 81 are powers of 3. The answers to the last questions asked by the problem are $81 \times 3 = 243$, and $243 + 121 = 364$.

The same principle applies no matter how far we want to take it, for the principle uses the formula

$$\sum_{k=0}^{n} 3^k = \frac{3^{n+1} - 1}{2},$$

which is readily proved by mathematical induction. Although this would be beyond the capabilities of general math students, it makes an easy problem for the algebra student who has studied mathematical induction.

177. a. 30¢, 30¢

b. 40¢, 40¢

c. 15¢, 20¢

d. 55¢, 60¢

e. $1.30, $1.30

178. A. a. 144 sq in., 1 sq ft

b. 81 sq in., 9/16 sq ft

B. a. Each tile is 1 ft in both length and width, so it will take 12 × 15 = 180 tiles.

b. We convert the floor's feet to inches to see how many 9-in. tiles we need each way. (12 × 12)/9 = 16, and (15 × 12)/9 = 20, so we need 16 × 20 = 320 tiles.

C. a. 11 × 11 = 121 tiles

b. (11 × 12)/9 = 14 2/3 tiles each way, leaving 1/3 tile unused from 15 tiles. We are not allowed to piece together two of the 1/3 tiles to make a 2/3 tile, so we need 15 tiles in each direction, or a total of 15 × 15 = 225 tiles. We might be tempted to think that the last corner (where the series of 2/3 pieces are meeting) is being covered twice this way and that we need only 224 tiles, but we can figure another way: Ignoring the extra 2/3 piece needed for a line of tile in each direction, we need 14 × 14 = 196 tiles that we aren't going to cut up. Now if we cut up two sets of 14 tiles each (to get our 2/3 tile needed in each direction) to complete the tiling along the two walls, the last corner is still bare, and we need a square piece of tile 6 in. × 6 in. for it, which means cutting up another whole piece. Our total is 196 + 28 + 1 = 225.

D. a. 180/12 = 15; 15 boxes

b. 320/12 = 26 2/3; 27 boxes

c. 121/12 = 10 1/12; 11 boxes

d. 225/12 = 18 3/4; 19 boxes

E. a. 180/20 = 9; 9 boxes × $25 = $225

b. 320/20 = 16; 16 boxes × $25 = $400

c. 121/20 = 6 1/20; 7 boxes × $25 = $175

d. 225/20 = 11 1/4; 12 boxes × $25 = $30(

F. The number of boxes doesn't change for answers **a–c**.

a. 9 boxes, $225, no discount

b. 16 boxes, $400 − 10% discount of $40 = $360

c. 7 boxes, $175, no discount

d. 13 boxes, $325 − 10% discount of $32.50 = $292.50

179. The area of the square is 6 in. × 6 in. = 36 sq in. The four triangles are congruent, and so each area is 1/4 of 36 sq in., or 9 sq in.

180. Parenthesized numbers refer to clue numbers in the problem.

Jessica doesn't own the Packard or the Studebaker (2) or the Hudson (5), so she owns the Kaiser.

Frampton isn't Bertram or Rex (4) or Gino (6), so he is Douglas. Then Jessica is not Frampton (5, Douglas) or Learned (2) or Edgewood (1, Kaiser), so she is MacArthur. The Learneds don't own the Packard or the Studebaker (2), so they own the Hudson. Gino is not Learned (3, Hudson) or MacArthur (3), so he is Edgewood.

Jessica MacArthur is not married to Bertram (7, Kaiser), so she is married to Rex. Then Bertram is Learned.

Gino doesn't have the Studebaker (3), so Douglas has it, and Gino has the Packard.

Cheryl isn't married to Gino (3) or to Douglas (3, Studebaker), so she is married to Bertram. Nora isn't married to Gino (1, Edgewood), so Anne is, and Nora is married to Douglas.

Anne and Gino Edgewood, Packard

Cheryl and Bertram Learned, Hudson

Jessica and Rex MacArthur, Kaiser

Nora and Douglas Frampton, Studebaker

181. Parenthesized numbers refer to clue numbers in the problem.

Jakar (7), Otphor (5), and Zadok (6) are men, so Kaliz, Telerp, and Umnak are women. The men's suns are Arcturus (8), Capella (10) and Vega (4), so the women's are Deneb, Procyon, and Sirius.

The force field user is a man (4) but is not the Vegan (4) or the Capellan (10), so he is from Arcturus. Then Xabot's enemy, who is male (10), is not from Arcturus (10, force field) or Capella (10), so he is the Vegan.

Zadok is not from Vega (6, Xabot) or Arcturus (8), so he is the Capellan. Then, since Jakar is not the Vegan (7), he is from Arcturus. Then Otphor is the Vegan. Since clue 7 mentions all three men, Xighu's enemy must then be the Capellan, Zadok.

From clue 9, Otphor's sun has 11 or 13 planets, but not 11 (3, female), so it has 13 planets. Then Umnak's sun and Sirius have 16 and 20 planets (9). Since Otphor is Xabot's enemy, clue 1 tells us that Kaliz' sun has 16 planets and the electroray user's sun has 20 planets. Combining clues 1 and 9, Umnak is the electroray user, 20 planets, and Kaliz' sun, Sirius, has 16 planets.

By elimination, Telerp's sun has 11 planets (3, female), and Jakar's and Zadok's suns have 9 and 10 planets. Now Xighu's enemy is Zadok, so (from clue 13), Zadok's sun has 10 planets. Jakar's sun has 9 planets, and Jakar's planet has a rose sky.

Since Otphor's sun has 13 planets, the planet with the blue sky belongs to the sun with 9, 10, or 11 planets (9), but not 9 (rose) and not 10 (8, Zadok), so it is one of 11 planets of Telerp's sun.

The planets with yellow and white skies are women's (2) and so have to be the planets of Kaliz and Umnak. Combining clue 11 with what we already have, we conclude that the planet with the white sky is Umnak's, and the one with the yellow sky is Kaliz'. Otphor's planet's sky is not lavender (5), so it is ivory, and Zadok's is lavender.

Procyon does not have 20 planets (14), so it is not Umnak's sun. So Procyon is Telerp's sun, and Deneb is Umnak's sun.

From clue 9, the sun of Xorbus' enemy has 9,

10, or 11 planets. It is not 11 (9, blue sky) or 10 (Xighu), so it is 9, and Xorbus' enemy is Jakar.

Xulloc is Umnak's enemy (12). Xydan is not Telerp's enemy (3, 11 planets), so Xydan is Kaliz' enemy, and Xenn is Telerp's enemy.

Telerp does not use the gravitron or the magnetor (14, Procyon) or the hyperscope (3, 11 planets), so she uses the neutronom.

The magnetor user's sun has 9 or 10 planets (14), but not 9 (force field), so it has 10.

Kaliz does not use the gravitron (2, yellow sky), so she uses the hyperscope, and Otphor uses the gravitron.

name	sex	sun	sky
Jakar	male	Arcturus	rose
Kaliz	female	Sirius	yellow
Otphor	male	Vega	ivory
Telerp	female	Procyon	blue
Umnak	female	Deneb	white
Zadok	male	Capella	lavender

planets	enemy	weapon
9	Xorbus	force field
16	Xydan	hyperscope
13	Xabot	gravitron
11	Xenn	neutronom
20	Xulloc	electroray
10	Xighu	magnetor

Pages 124–129

182. Four answers are possible because 1-A and 1-D can be exchanged, as can 4-D and 5-A.

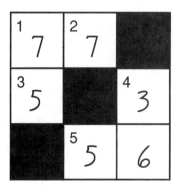

183. Two answers are possible because 1-A and 1-D can be exchanged.

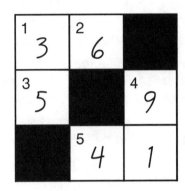

184. This is not possible. There are only four two-digit answers, and two of these (1-A and 1-D) must start with the same digit, while the other two (4-D and 5-A) must end with the same digit. If we pair 47 and 48, then 17 and 35 do not make a pair. If we pair 47 and 17, then 48 and 35 do not make a pair. This exhausts the possibilities, since 47 and 35 cannot be paired.

185. The story tells us that the first digits of 4-A, 3-D, and 8-D are 1. Then (because the only multiple of 3 that ends in 1 is $3 \times 7 = 21$) 2-A implies that 4-A ends in 7, which forces 4-A, 2-A, and 10-A. For part of 1-D, we need 4-A × 8-D = 17 × 16 = 272. The teenagers are different ages, so (because we know 4-A and 8-D) Eleanor's age is 13, 14, 15, 18, or 19, and 1-D says one of these × 272 has 1 as the second digit. Only 272 × 19 gives this result, so 3-D is 19 and 1-D is 5168. This forces 7-A and fills in all squares.

186. The story implies that 11-D and 6-A are 1 and 4 or 2 and 8. This means that 10-A must end in

1 or 2 and so can't be $4 \times 4 = 16$. So 10-A is 4 × 8 = 32, forcing 6-A, 11-D, 8-D, and 7-A. 5-D ends in 4, so 1-D implies that 5-D is 34, 44, 54 ..., or 94. 7-A and 1-D imply that 32 + the square of 5-D must have 4 as the third digit. O our possible values for 5-D, only 54 gives this result. This forces 5-D, 1-D, and 2-A, and fills in all squares.

These grids work like crossword puzzle grids, except that digits, rather than letters, are written in the squares.

The first three problems are simply to give the students the experience of using the grid correctly. The other problems are fun to solve and teach the students that the logical place to start a solution is not necessarily at the first clue one encounters. They also teach that one may have to consider and discard various choices before finding one that satisfies all conditions.

The arithmetic involved can make the problem tedious, overshadowing the enjoyment of discovering a workable sequence of clues to follow. To circumvent this, encourage the use of hand calculators.

Pages 130–132

187. a. 25

b. 30

c. 75

Red tape, because he'd heard his parents say that all government bureaus are full of red tape.

188. 2 o'clock

189. 8 o'clock

190. 6 o'clock

91. 6 o'clock

92. 3 o'clock

93. 5 o'clock

94. 3 o'clock

95. 3 o'clock

Page 133

Make sure the students understand these simple ideas. We're going to expand them into modular arithmetic and also use the ideas to support understanding of number bases other than base ten.

96. 6 o'clock

97. 4 o'clock

98. 5 o'clock

99. 2 o'clock

100. 5 o'clock

101. 1 o'clock

Page 134

102. a. Yes. When going forward, the clock counts 1, 2, ..., 6 and then starts at 1 again, in effect discarding the first 6 numbers, and that's what Mario's method does. When going backward, the clock counts 6, 5, ..., 1, and then starts at 6 again, in effect adding 6 each time the next number would be less than 1. Again, that's what Mario's method does.

    b. 1) He would use 9's instead of 6's.

    2) Yes. The principle is the same as explained in part **a** above for the 6-hour clock.

    c. Same as **b(2)** above.

Make sure the students understand exactly how Mario does the problems. His method is much easier than counting out the hours one by one on the fingers. Also, it will help avoid mistakes, because some students, when asked for the time 5 hours after 10 o'clock (on a 12-hour clock) will start with 10 and count 10 (one), 11 (two), 12 (three), 1 (four), 2 (five), getting an answer of 2 o'clock.

Left to devise their own arithmetic notation for, say a 12-hour clock, students are likely to write something like "9 + 7 = 16 − 12 = 4." Do not allow

such an incorrect use of "=." Offer an acceptable alternative such as

$$9 + 7 = 16; 16 − 12 = 4.$$

If your students can work with negative numbers, lead them to discover that negative numbers can be used to solve some clock arithmetic problems. For instance, consider Mario's second example:

> "Or say it's 1 o'clock and I want 3 hours ago. If I take 1 − 3, I'll get less than 1, so I add 6 first. I take 1 + 6 − 3 and get 4, so the answer is 4 o'clock."

When Mario found $1 − 3 < 1$, he stopped long enough to add 6 to the 1 so that he would get a positive result. If he knew how to use negative numbers, he could get $1 − 3 = -2$, which isn't on the clock face, and then add 6 to get his answer of 4. This method computes $1 − 3 + 6$ instead of $1 + 6 − 3$.

While that example doesn't show much difference in effort expended, the use of negative numbers can be handy when the students start using a 24-hour clock two pages from now. To find the time 22 hours before 5 P.M., the method shown there has them figuring this way:

$5 + 12 = 17; 17 − 22$ is negative, so add 24 to 17; $24 + 17 = 41$; then $41 − 22 = 19.$

We see some good possibilities for computation errors there. Using negative numbers, the figuring would be:

$$5 + 12 = 17; 17 − 22 = -5; -5 + 24 = 19.$$

Pages 135–138

203. a. Yes. We already know that Mario's method always works. The only difference between his method and Choon-Wei's is that Mario does the problem while working with a large number to be added or subtracted, afterwards reducing the answer by multiples of 6, while Choon-Wei reduces the large numbers to be added or subtracted before doing the problem. The two methods give identical results.

    b. She would find $15 − 7 − 7 = 1$ and add that to 2, getting an answer of 3 o'clock.

    c. Yes. Mario's method works for all clocks

and, as explained in part **a** above, Choon-Wei's method gives the same results.

204. 10 A.M.

205. 1 P.M.

206. 7 P.M.

207. 2 A.M.

208. 9 A.M.

209. This is OK if we keep our heads screwed on straight while we're doing it, but it leaves room for careless mistakes. If we're going to figure answers as suggested, then we have to follow these rules:

a. An answer of 24, or answers from 1 through 11 will be

1) A.M. if the starting hour was A.M.

2) P.M. if the starting hour was P.M.

b. Answers from 12 through 23 will be

1) A.M. if the starting hour was P.M.

2) P.M. if the starting hour was A.M.

For example, to compute 14 hours after 3 P.M., we would take 3 + 14, get 17, and have to remember that this will designate an A.M. hour in this case, since we started with a P.M. hour.

210. 1700

211. 1300

212. 1200

213. 2000

214. 0100

215. 0150

Pages 139–140

Other calculations can be correct. For example, I might show an answer of $6 - 8 + 9 \equiv 7$ (mod 9), and either of these (and more) other answers would be equally correct: $6 - 8 + 9 = 7 \equiv 7$ (mod 9); $6 - 8 + 45 = 43 \equiv 7$ (mod 9). Make sure that any number added (in order to counteract a negative result) is a multiple of the modulus. If the students can work with negative numbers, they might also show this answer: $6 - 8 = -2 \equiv 7$ (mod 9).

216. $7 + 30 = 37 \equiv 1$ (mod 9)

217. $5 + 8 = 13 \equiv 1$ (mod 6)

218. $5 - 8 + 6 \equiv 3$ (mod 6)

219. $3 - 11 + 10 \equiv 2$ (mod 5)

220. $8 + 24 = 32 \equiv 2$ (mod 10)

221. $3 + 10 = 13 \equiv 1$ (mod 2)

222. $6 - 15 + 16 = 7 \equiv 7$ (mod 16)

In mathematics, the symbol "$\equiv$" usually means "is identical with" or "is identically equal to." However, in statements such as

$$15 \equiv 3 \text{ (mod 12)},$$

"$\equiv$" is read as "is congruent to."

Students at this level associate congruence with geometric figures and the symbol "$\cong$" rather than with numbers and the symbol "$\equiv$," and you may have to explain to them that mathematical entities other than geometric figures can have congruence relations and that "$\equiv$" is used for any congruence relation of the form

$$a \equiv b \text{ (mod } c).$$

Entities that can have this kind of congruence relation include integers (which we will now be working with), complex numbers, polynomials, and members of a group.

The problem $15 \equiv ?$ (mod 12) has an infinite number of answers, all of the form $12n + 3$, where is any integer. Although modular arithmetic, which what we are studying at the moment, limits the acceptable answers to $0 \le ? < 12$, our clock goes from 1 to 12 rather than from 0 to 11, and our answers will be in the range $0 < ? \le 12$.

Pages 141–143

Although the final answers must be the one shown, the calculations may differ.

223. $1 + 7 = 8 \equiv 2$ (mod 6)

224. $3 - 5 \equiv 4$ (mod 6)

225. $5 + 13 \equiv 0$ (mod 6)

226. $0 + 11 \equiv 5$ (mod 6)

227. $2 - 10 \equiv 4$ (mod 6)

228. $4 + 45 = 49 \equiv 1$ (mod 6)

229. $4 - 45 + 48 = 7 \equiv 1$ (mod 6)

230. $39 - (25 + 4) = 39 - 29 = 10 \equiv 4$ (mod 6)

231. $4 \times 8 - 20 = 32 - 20 = 12 \equiv 0$ (mod 6)

232. $3^2 + 16 = 9 + 16 = 25 \equiv 1$ (mod 6)

233. 3 less than the product of 2 and $8 = 2 \times 8 - 3$ $13 \equiv 1$ (mod 6)

234. $8 + 11 = 19 \equiv 4$ (mod 5)

235. $4 + 29 - 17 = 16 \equiv 2$ (mod 7)

236. $3 \times 6 + 10 - 4 = 18 + 10 - 4 = 24 \equiv 4$ (mod 10)

237. $29 - 22 - 10 = 7 - 10 \equiv 2$ (mod 5)

238. $12 + 2 - 19 = 14 - 19 \equiv 3$ (mod 4)

Encourage the students to try several examples in order to convince themselves that they can use exactly the same computations with this clock that they used for a 6-hour clock whose numbers were 1–6, except that whenever they would have had an answer of 6, they will now have an answer of 0. Make sure they understand that this applies only to a final answer—i.e., that they still have to add or subtract multiples of 6, not 0, when doing their computations. For example, 19 hours after 2 o'clock, it will be $2 + 19 - 6 - 6 - 6 = 3$ o'clock. This is more clearly shown by

$$2 + 19 = 21 \equiv 3 \text{ (mod 6)}.$$

If your students can work with negative numbers, ask them if they could have a 6-hour clock whose numbers were -1, 0, 1, 2, 3, 4. Let them discuss the idea and try out some problems for it. [The answer is yes. In this case, we would be replacing 5 with -1, and since $-1 \equiv 5$ (mod 6), this is a workable idea. Just as intermediate computations were not affected by replacing 6 with 0, so they will not be affected by replacing 5 with -1. For example, to find the time 21 hours after 2 o'clock, we would compute $2 + 21 = 23 \equiv -1$ (mod 6) instead of $2 + 21 = 23 \equiv 5$ (mod 6).]

Pages 144–146

239. $(18 - 3)/5 = 15/5 = 3$, so $18 \equiv 3$ (mod 5)

240. $(13 - 7)/3 = 6/3 = 2$, so $7 \equiv 13$ (mod 3)

241. $25 - 20 = 5$; $(16 - 5)/12 = 11/12$, so $25 - 20 \not\equiv 16$ (mod 12)

242. $(7 \times 8 - 4 \times 8)/6 = (56 - 32)/6 = 24/6 = 4$, so $7 \times 8 \equiv 4 \times 8$ (mod 6)

243. $17 - 12 + 20 = 5 + 20 = 25$; $(25 - 11)/7 = 14/7 = 2$, so $17 - 12 + 20 \equiv 11$ (mod 7)

244. $23 + 12 = 35$; $3 \times 5 + 3^2 = 15 + 9 = 24$; $(35 - 24)/11 = 11/11 = 1$, so $23 + 12 \equiv 3 \times 5 + 3^2$ (mod 11)

245. $14 + 16/4 = 14 + 4 = 18$; $4 \times 2 = 8$; $(18 - 8)/10 = 1$, so $14 + 16/4 \equiv 4 \times 2$ (mod 10)

246. $(4 \times 6 + 3 \times 12)/4 = (24 + 36)/4 = 60/4 = 15$; $15 \times 3 - 4 \times 10 = 45 - 40 = 5$; $(15 - 5)/8 = 10/8$, so $(4 \times 6 + 3 \times 12)/4 \not\equiv 15 \times 3 - 4 \times 10$ (mod 8)

Point out that the use of letters in $a \equiv b$ (mod c) does not suggest that the students either are expected to understand algebra or are about to be taught algebra. The letters are used simply as a convenient way to make a general statement, and it is understood that numbers will replace the letters for each specific case.

The letters are variables, of course, but I wouldn't call them that in a general math class. Such students more readily accept a "letter" than a "variable" as a placeholder for a number.

Some students may be confused by the use of a, b, and c regardless of how splendid, lucid, brilliant, skillful, and ingenious your explanation is when you make it perfectly obvious that the letters are there merely to show the students where to put the numbers they will be using. In this case, consider replacing a, b, and c with, say a triangle, a square, and a circle, and show the class how the numbers, once known, can be written inside these figures. For some reason, students who can't grasp the idea of replacing the letters with numbers are perfectly willing to accept the idea of writing numbers inside the geometric figures.

The numbers used for a, b, and c do not have to be distinct. Any two, or even all three, can be the same number, except that c cannot be 0, since it has to be able to divide $a - b$.

Most students will take for granted that solving a congruence problem is analogous to solving a clock arithmetic problem even though the problem doesn't mention a clock. However, some students may not take this mental step, and it wouldn't hurt to point out to the class that the modulus in a congruence problem is analogous to the number of hours on a clock in a clock arithmetic problem and that the two kinds of problems are solved in the same way.

Page 147

The "yes" or "no" answers are correct, but the students may find other examples.

247. No. Suppose the common factor is 3.

    a. Put $a = 12$, $b = 9$, $c = 6$.

    b. Put $a = 12$, $b = 9$, $c = 5$.

248. a. No. Put $a = 15$, $b = 3$, $c = 4$.

    b. No. Put $a = 7$, $b = 3$, $c = 4$.

    c. Yes. Put $a = 14$, $b = 8$, $c = 3$.

Pages 148–156

These are not trivial problems for general math students, and it is assumed that students who try to do them have a good understanding of the material preceding these problems.

Remind the students that we are working only with integers, so we don't have to consider what to do if, say, given $a \equiv b$ (mod c), a is a fraction.

Also remind them that parentheses around terms of an expression are sometimes unnecessary—e.g., $(r - s) - t = r - s - t$—but stress that parentheses cannot be used indiscriminately—e.g., $(r - s) - t \neq r - (s - t)$.

Students can recite a definition and understand it thoroughly without ever thinking of using it to prove something. Point out to them that if they are given $a \equiv b$ (mod c), they can use it to prove that $(a - b)/c$ is an integer, and conversely, if $(a - b)/c$ is an integer, they can use that fact to prove $a \equiv b$ (mod c).

Aside from counterexamples to false statements, the answers given here for most problems are divided into three parts:

1) "Setup" shows the setup for the other two parts of the proof. Although this looks (and is) algebraic, the congruences are exactly like the general form shown in the textbook, and the students should be able to do this much on their own or, at worst, understand the setup if you decide to start them off by showing them this part of the proof.

2) "Algebra" shows the proof that might be done by a student who understands elementary algebra.

3) "Students" shows a proof the students might use if they have no knowledge of algebra or of what to do with a negative number. You may notice that steps are sometimes skipped. For example, a student (without algebra) who wants twice as much as $a - b$ is unlikely to write this in the form of the distributive principle—i.e., $2(a - b) = 2a - 2b$. Instead, the student is more likely to reason that if there was one a before, then there will be two a's now, and if there was one b subtracted before, then the subtraction will be for two b's now. The result of this reasoning is likely to be written without any intermediate steps—i.e., twice as much as $a - b$ is $2a - 2b$ or is $a + a - b - b$.

Page 148

Part **a** proves that congruence is a reflexive relation.

249. Setup: Given for parts **a** and **b**. For part **c**, $nc \equiv 0$ (mod c).

Algebra:

a. $a - a = 0$, and since c divides 0, c also divides $a - a$. By definition, then, $a \equiv a$ (mod c).

b. $c - 0 = c$, which is divisible by c, so by definition $c \equiv 0$ (mod c).

c. $nc - 0 = nc$, which is divisible by c, so by definition $nc \equiv 0$ (mod c).

Students:

a. When a number is subtracted from itself, the result is 0. Any modulus divides 0, so (by definition) any number is congruent to itself.

b–c. Any number $- 0 =$ that number, and any integer will divide any multiple of itself. The modulus is an integer, so the conclusions follow by definition.

Page 149

250. Setup: Given.

Algebra: We're given $a \equiv b$ (mod c), so by definition, $(a - b)/c$ is an integer. Then (from "Free info") $(b - a)/c$ is an integer, so $b \equiv a$ (mod c) by definition.

Students: Same as "Algebra."

251. Setup: Given.

Algebra:

a. By definition, we're given that c divides both $a - b$ and $b - d$, so c will also divide their sum, $a - b + b - d = (a - b + b) - d =$ (from problem 64b) $[a - (b - b)] - d = [a - 0] - d = a - d$. This defines $a \equiv d$ (mod c).

b. This proof is analogous to the proof for part **a**, except take the difference instead of the sum.

Students:

a. By definition, we're given that c divides both $a - b$ and $b - d$, so c will also divide their sum, $a - b + b - d = a - d$ (because if you subtract b and then add it back again, you get what you started with, *a*). This is the definition of $a \equiv d \pmod{c}$.

   b. Problem 250 says the second part of the given data, $d \equiv b \pmod{c}$, can be turned around to $b \equiv d \pmod{c}$. This makes the problem exactly like part **a**.

Problem 250 proves that congruence is a symmetric relation. Part **a** of problem 251 proves that congruence is a transitive relation. These two problems, along with problem 249a, establish that congruence between integers is an **equivalence** relation—i.e., (1) the relation is reflexive, symmetric, and transitive, and (2) given a modulus, any two integers are either congruent or not congruent.

Pages 150–154

252. Setup: Prove: If $a \equiv b \pmod{c}$, then

   a. 2 times $a \equiv 2$ times $b \pmod{c}$.

   b. if *n* is integral, then *n* times $a \equiv n$ times $b \pmod{c}$.

   Algebra:

   a. By definition, we are given $(a - b)/c = m$ for some integer *m*. Then $2(a - b)/c = 2m$, and $2m$ is also an integer. The equation can be rewritten as $(2a - 2b)/c = 2m$, so by definition, $2a \equiv 2b \pmod{c}$.

   b. The proof is analogous to the proof for part **a**, except use *n* here instead of 2 there.

   Students:

   a. We are given $a \equiv b \pmod{c}$, so *c* goes into *a* − *b* a whole number of times. But if it does that, then it goes into twice as much twice as many times. This means that *c* goes into 2 times *a* − 2 times *b*, so (by definition) 2 times $a \equiv 2$ times $b \pmod{c}$.

   b. This proof is analogous to the part **a** proof. Use "*n* times" here for "twice" there, and use "*n*" here for "2" there.

253. Notice that to start the solution by using the definition of congruence will result in trying to evaluate either $[(3 - 22) - 7]/4$ or $[7 - (3 - 22)]/4$, which ordinarily can't be done without a knowledge of negative numbers. Since negative numbers are forbidden for this problem, a different approach must be found.

One way to do the problem is to remember what we did before we had the definition of

congruence—i.e., when we had a negative number, we added some multiple of the modulus in order to have an equivalent (with respect to the modulus) positive number, and if we had a positive number *n* greater than the modulus, we reduced it until $0 \leq n <$ modulus:

$$3 - 22 \equiv 3 - 22 + 20 = 1 \pmod{4}$$

$$7 \equiv 7 - 4 = 3 \pmod{4}$$

Referring back to clock arithmetic, we know that a 4-hour clock cannot show times of 1 o'clock and 3 o'clock simultaneously, so the given numbers are not congruent.

A second way to do the problem is to use indirect proof, along with problem 64b at the top of the textbook page:

Suppose $7 \equiv 3 - 22 \pmod{4}$. Then [definition] 4 divides $7 - (3 - 22) =$ [problem 64b] $(7 - 3) + 22 = 4 + 22 = 26$. But this is a contradiction, because 4 doesn't divide 26. Therefore, our assumption must be wrong, and so $7 \not\equiv 3 - 22 \pmod{4}$.

254. Setup: Given.

Algebra: In order not to interrupt continuity, steps going from $(a - b) + (e - f)$ to $a - b + e - f$ and from there to $(a + e) - (b + f)$ have been omitted in the proof for part **a** below. If you would rather your students included such steps, we could go from $(a - b) + (e - f)$ to $(a + e) - (b + f)$ in various ways. One way would be to use problems 64c and 64a and the commutative property of addition. Another way would be to change all starting subtractions to additions of -1 times the numbers, use the associative and commutative properties of addition along with the distributive property of addition over multiplication, and then change the -1 multiplications back to subtractions.

   a. By definition, there are integers *m* and *n* such that the two given congruences can be written as $(a - b)/c = m$, and $(e - f)/c = n$. Then $m + n$ (which is also an integer) $= (a - b)/c + (e - f)/c = (a - b + e - f)/c = [(a + e) - (b + f)]/c$. Then (by definition) $a + e \equiv b + f \pmod{c}$.

b. The proof is analogous to the proof for the first conclusion, except compute $m - n$ (the difference between two integers is an integer) instead of $m + n$.

Students:

a. By definition, we're given that $(a - b)/c$ and $(e - f)/c$ are integers, so we'll get an integer when we add them. When two fractions have the same denominator, they are added by adding the numerators and leaving the denominator alone. In the given fractions, each numerator has a number to start with and a number to be subtracted, so if we add these numerators, we'll have two numbers to be subtracted from the sum of the two starting numbers. Then the numerator will be $a + e - b - f =$ (problem 64a) $(a + e) - (b + f)$. The denominator is still c, so (by definition) $a + e \equiv b + f \pmod{c}$.

b. The first part is analogous to part **a**, except that we subtract instead of add. Then $a - b - (e - f) =$ (problem 64b) $a - b - e + f =$ (problem 64d) $a - e - b + f =$ (problem 64b) $a - e - (b - f) = (a - e) - (b - f)$. This means (by definition) that $a - e \equiv b - f \pmod{c}$.

255. For parts **a** and **b**, apply problem 254 to the given congruence along with problem 249c. For parts **c** and **d**, apply problem 250 to problem 249c and then proceed as for parts **a** and **b**. To prove parts **e–h**, apply problem 254 to part **c** or part **d** along with problem 249c.

256. Use problem 249a to get $n \equiv n \pmod{c}$. Using this, along with the given congruence, apply problem 254. (We have two congruences here and two in problem 254. Each congruence here can be either congruence of problem 254.)

257. a. No. Put $f = 3$, $a = 27$, $b = 15$, $c = 4$.

b. No. Put $f = 6$, $a = 42$, $b = 12$, $c = 5$.

258. a. [This is not an easy problem for general math students.] Yes. We're given (by definition) that c divides $a - b$, so every factor of c has to divide $a - b$. In particular, f divides $a - b$, so $a \equiv b \pmod{f}$ and (problem 250) $b \equiv a \pmod{f}$. We're given that a is of the form fn, but (problem 249c) $fn \equiv 0 \pmod{f}$, which means $a \equiv 0 \pmod{f}$. It follows that (prob-

lem 251b) $b \equiv 0 \pmod{f}$, so (definition of $\equiv$) f divides $b - 0 = b$, which is another way of saying that f is a factor of b.

b. Yes. Saying "a multiple of a prime number" is the same as saying "not a prime number." Put the common factor $= 6$, $a = 30$, $b = 6$, $c = 12$.

Pages 155–156

259. The answers given here are specific enough to allow you to see how the problems could be solved, but they are not detailed enough for a proof submitted by a student. [Not all correct answers to the questions asked are provable by general math students, but the students may enjoy trying to prove them.]

A. a. No. Put $f = 3$, $a = 21$, $b = 6$, $c = 5$.

b. Not necessarily. Put $f = 3$, $a = 21$, $b = 9$, $c = 6$.

c–d. Yes. We're given (by definition) that c is a factor of $a - b$, which, in turn, is a factor of $a^n - b^n$ for any integer $n > 0$.

e. Not necessarily. Put $a = 7$, $b = 4$, $c = 3$.

B. a. Yes. Use problem 250 on $d \equiv e \pmod{c}$. Apply problem 254 to that result and $a \equiv b \pmod{c}$.

b. Yes. By definition, there are integers m, n such that $m = (a - b)/c$, $n = (d - e)/c$. Multiply both sides by c and add the last term to both sides: $mc + b = a$, $nc + e = d$. Now $ad = (mc + b)(nc + e) = mc(nc + e) + b(nc + e) = c(mnc + me + bn) + be$, so $(ad - be)/c = mnc + me + bn$, an integer, and (by definition of $\equiv$) $ad \equiv be \pmod{c}$.

c. Yes. Apply problem 250 to $d \equiv e \pmod{c}$. The proof is now analogous to the proof for part **b**.

d. Not necessarily. Put $a = 60$, $b = 42$, $c = 6$, $d = 15$, $e = 21$.

C. a–b. Not necessarily. Put $a = 3$, $b = 7$, $c = 2$, $d = 18$, $e = 3$, $f = 5$.

This is an open-ended problem. The questions asked in the textbook are only a few of the many that might be asked. For maximum effect, do a brainstorming session with the class. Here is how you could do it effectively:

Partition your chalkboard into four sections. Head the sections

    A. If $a \equiv b$ (mod c), then _____ .

    B. If $a \equiv b$ (mod c) and $d \equiv e$ (mod c), then _____ .

    C. If $a \equiv b$ (mod c) and $d \equiv e$ (mod f), then _____ .

    D. If _____ , then $a \equiv b$ (mod c).

Tell the students to think of ways the blanks might be filled in. Here are the rules for the students:

- Don't bother to raise your hand.

- Call out whatever occurs to you. At this point, we don't care whether or not it's true, so don't stop to think about it first.

- Don't make comments about conjectures already made. Such comments interrupt the trend of thought, diverting it toward solving a problem rather than toward thinking of new ones.

- "Tailgating" is permitted. Don't feel that you are stealing someone else's idea if you want to modify it or if it makes you think of a related idea. Call out your conjecture.

Appoint two recording secretaries. Number each conjecture (1, 2, ... for each section A–D) as you quickly write it on the chalkboard. One secretary will record the even-numbered conjectures, and the other will record the odd-numbered ones. Each secretary will have four sheets of paper, one for each section.

It is best to concentrate on one section at a time. Start with section A. When the students are running out of ideas, move to section B. While the class is working on section B, a student might think of an additional conjecture for section A. Allow this.

At the end of the class period, collect the eight sheets from the two secretaries. Take the eight lists home (because your designated class preparation hour won't give you enough time) and make four masters (one for each of sections A–D) to be dittoed or otherwise reproduced. Distribute copies to the class the next day so that everyone has a list of the problems to be considered.

Pages 157–170

Students tend to be confused when, after having been carefully taught to distinguish between numer-

als and numbers, they read a sentence such as, "What are the factors of 12?" It's obvious to them that 12 is a numeral, and a numeral is just something made from a given set of symbols, so how can a numeral have factors? Or maybe the factors are the symbols that make up the numeral, and so the factors of 12 are 1 and 2?

A different, but related, question is raised in the students' minds when they read, "What are the factors of the number 12?" because now they read that the symbol "12" is no longer a numeral but has suddenly become a number, which they know is not possible. So perhaps the question should be, "What are the factors of the number represented by the numeral 12?" That seems to be a complicated way to ask what should be a simple question.

The textbook avoids such difficulties by saying "number" when referring either to a numeral or to a number. This is correct usage according to the dictionary, and the students are not confused, for they judge by context (as they do for so many other words).

Pages 157–160

260. 24

261. 27

262. 26

263. 65

264. 167

265. 57

266. 60

267. 353

268. 2560

269. 179

The concepts in Part I of the lesson are so well known that the students may tend to skim through the material, thinking it too elementary for them. To know something and to understand it thoroughly, however, are two different things, and what we want is for the students to understand these ideas so well that they will be able to apply analogous reasoning to number bases other than base ten.

The value of our written numbers depends on both the base used and the place a digit occupies. The definition of a "base n number system" includes the stipulation of place value for each digit.

Our way of writing numbers is sometimes called

a "base and place number system." Not all number systems use the concept of base and place. For example, Roman numerals (how many digits are there?) do not have a place value. "XI" = 11, and "XC" = 90, showing that "X" takes a value of 10 one time and a value of -10 another time, even though it is in the same place both times.

Pages 161–163

The answers here are given in two parts: (1) base eight and the base ten conversion; (2) base eleven and the base ten conversion.

270. 1) base eight, 326 + 6 = 334; base ten, 214 + 6 = 220

2) base eleven, 326 + 6 = 331; base ten, 391 + 6 = 397

271. 1) base eight, 134 + 56 = 212; base ten, 92 + 46 = 138

2) base eleven, 134 + 56 = 18A; base ten, 158 + 61 = 219

272. 1) base eight, 175 + 67 = 264; base ten, 125 + 55 = 180

2) base eleven, 175 + 67 = 231; base ten, 203 + 73 = 276

273. 1) base eight, 475 + 65 = 562; base ten, 317 + 53 = 370

2) base eleven, 475 + 65 = 52A; base ten, 566 + 71 = 637

274. 1) base eight, 364 + 427 = 1013; base ten, 244 + 279 = 523

2) base eleven, 364 + 427 = 790; base ten, 433 + 513 = 946

275. 1) base eight, 777 + 777 = 1776; base ten, 511 + 511 = 1022

2) base eleven, 777 + 777 = 1443; base ten, 931 + 931 = 1862

276. 1) base eight, 1000 + 500 = 1500; base ten, 512 + 320 = 832

2) base eleven, 1000 + 500 = 1500; base ten, 1331 + 605 = 1936

277. 1) base eight, 6354 + 4756 = 13332; base ten, 3308 + 2542 = 5850

2) base eleven, 6354 + 4756 = AAAA; base ten, 8408 + 6232 = 14640

We want the students to concentrate on thinking about how addition (and, later, subtraction and multiplication) works in base ten and to use analogous reasoning in order to operate in other bases.

However, it's easy to get bogged down in the multiplication and subtraction needed for converting between base ten and other bases. What should be a stimulating critical thinking activity then becomes nine parts tedious busywork and only one part critical thinking.

Encourage the use of hand calculators for these problems.

Pages 164–173

278. In base eight, 500 is 5/8 of 1000, not 1/2 of 1000. So when we convert 1000_{eight} to 512_{ten}, we need to take 5/8 of 512 = 320 to get the base ten equivalent of 500_{eight}.

279. a. 39

b. 42

c. 169

d. 171

e. 683

f. 4095

280. 230

281. 434

282. 2301

283. 21124

284. 113

285. 117

286. 1001101

287. 658

288. 18B7

289. 1A2E

290. $33_{four} = 15_{ten} = 30_{five}$

291. $221_{three} = 25_{ten} = 41_{six}$

292. $244_{five} = 74_{ten} = 112_{eight}$

293. $2222_{four} = 170_{ten} = AA_{sixteen}$

294. $2222_{sixteen} = 8738_{ten} = 2020202_{four}$

295. $1324_{sixteen} = 4900_{ten} = 2A04_{twelve}$

296. $1001010_{two} = 74_{ten} = 1022_{four}$

297. base eight, $65 - 42 = 23$; base ten, $53 - 34 = 19$

298. base twelve, $65 - 42 = 23$; base ten, $77 - 50 = 27$

299. base eight, $65 - 47 = 16$; base ten, $53 - 39 = 14$

300. base sixteen, $65 - 47 = 1E$; base ten, $101 - 71 = 30$

301. base sixteen, $CB - AC = 1F$; base ten, $203 - 172 = 31$

302. base two, $10011010 - 1011001 = 1000001$; base ten, $154 - 89 = 65$

303. base four, $2122 - 1121 = 1001$; base ten, $154 - 89 = 65$

304. a–b. Yes. They would work analogously to the other bases we've discussed.

    c. No, for two reasons. First, how could we show both 0 and 1, if we had only one digit available? Second, in order to have a base n number system, n must take on different values for different powers, which 1 does not do. For example, each digit in a base ten number takes its own value times some power of ten.

305. Problems made up will vary. Let the students check each other's work. If any of the students know how to program a computer, offer extra credit for a (working!) program that will accept numbers in other bases and compute the answers in those other bases.

To multiply in other bases, I use the same method that I use for adding and subtracting in other bases. That is, I think in base ten and convert to and from base ten to get the answers.

For example, I solve the base twelve problem 47×3 like this: In base ten, $7 \times 3 = 21$, which is $12 + 9$, so enter 9 and carry 1. $4 \times 3 = 12$; $12 + 1$ (carried) $= 13$, which is $12 + 1$, or 11 in base twelve. So the answer is 119 in base twelve.

306. A twelve-inch by eighteen-inch rectangle has an inside border two inches wide. What is the area of the border and of the rectangle inside it? [The area of the outer rectangle is 12 in. × 18 in. = 216 sq in. To find the dimensions of the inner rectangle, we subtract 4 in. (because

the border is 2 in. wide at each end of the rectangle as well as at both top and bottom) from each dimension, getting 8 in. × 14 in. = 112 sq in. The border's area is the difference between these two areas, 104 sq in. Ask the students why, since the border is 2 in. wide and runs the length and width of the outer rectangle, we can't find its area by doubling 2 in. × 12 in. + 2 in. × 18 in. = doubling 24 sq in. + 36 sq in. = 2 × 60 sq in. = 120 sq in. (The answer is that the border's area at each corner of the rectangle has been counted twice. These "corner" areas, each 2 in. × 2 in., a total of 16 sq in., must then be subtracted—i.e., 120 sq in. − 16 sq in. = 104 sq in., the correct answer.)

307. 6 minutes

308. 6

309. 9.7

310. a. 9.2

    b. 8.8

    c. 10.0

    d. 8.1

    e. 9.5

    f. 10.9

    g. 11.7

    h. 4.3

    i. 4.9

    j. 4.7

    k. 5.1

Pages 174–176

311. 9×43

312. 4, 7

313. 21

314. 1, 1, 2, 3, 5, 8, 13, 21, 34, 55 (This is part of the Fibonacci series.)

315. 3125 ($1^1, 2^2, 3^3, 4^4, 5^5$)

316. 405 (Multiply by 3/2.)

317. $112 + 112 = 224$ (base five)

318. $5 \times 5 = 19$ (hexadecimal, or base sixteen)

319. 21, 34, 55, 89 (Pattern: start with 1, 1; add the previous two numbers.) This is the famous

Fibonacci series, which has many interesting properties. It would make a good investigative project for some of the more inquisitive students.

320. 19, 10, 20, 31 (Pattern: add 1, add 2, subtract 3, add 4, add 5, subtract 6, and so on.)

321. 38, 39, 78, 75 (Pattern: add 1, double, subtract 3, double.)

322. 26, 78, 71, 63 (Pattern: add 1, add 2, triple, subtract 3, subtract 4, triple, add 5, add 6, and so on.)

323. 18, 54, 27, 54 (Pattern: double, triple, take half.)

Finding patterns is an important aspect of mathematical development. Most answers will probably agree with the simple patterns shown in the answers below. However, students are used to having only one correct solution to a problem and may assume that an answer must be wrong if it doesn't agree with everyone else's answer, so do encourage those who found different patterns to tell the others about them. This will not only reassure such students but will also demonstrate to the rest of the class that there can, indeed, be more than one logical answer to some kinds of problems.

There can be more than one correct explanation for a given answer, and the students should be asked for their lines of reasoning. For example, given the sequence 2, 4, 6, 8, one person may think that each successive term is obtained by adding 2, while another might think that every term is obtained by counting what term it is (2 is term no. 1, 4 is term no. 2, and so on) and doubling the term number. Both people will list 10, 12, 14, 16 as the next four terms.

Page 177

This is another Diophantine problem.

324. (This is a hard problem.)

Along with 70 pounds of chicken, they could buy pounds of steak, roast, ham, and pollock, respectively: 5, 0, 20, 5; 18, 0, 8, 4; 12, 5, 12, 1; 3, 6, 20, 1.

With 75 pounds of chicken, the other quantities could be: 8, 0, 8, 9; 2, 5, 12, 6; 15, 5, 0, 5; 6, 6, 8, 5; 1, 8, 12, 4; 14, 8, 0, 3; 5, 9, 8, 3; 0, 11, 12, 2; 13, 11, 0, 1; 4, 12, 8, 1.

With 80 pounds of chicken, they could also buy: 5, 5, 0, 10; 4, 8, 0, 8; 3, 11, 0, 6; 2, 14, 0, 4; 1, 17, 0, 2.

Page 178

325. a. We need to find the prime factors of 2, 3, 4, 5, 6, and 7 and then eliminate any unneeded duplications. The prime factors are, respectively: 2; 3; 2, 2; 5; 2, 3; 7.

Although the prime factors of 4 are 2 and 2, we need both of these 2's in order to get 4. None of the numbers has more than two 2's so we can keep two 2's and eliminate the others. Also, no number has more than one 3 as a prime factor, so we need keep only one 3. Then the factors we will keep are 2, 2, 3, 5, and 7. The least number Lincoln car be thinking of is the product of these, 420.

b. No. The number is divisible by 4, and since $8 = 2 \times 4$, the number must have a remainder either of 0 or 4 when divided by 8. Expressing it algebraically, the number is of the form $4a$ and will always equal $dq + r$, where d is the divisor, q is the quotient, and r is the remainder, $0 \le r < d$. The problem asks about using 8 as the divisor, so we must have $4a = 8q + r$. Since 4 divides $8q$, i also has to divide r, and the only numbers in the required range are 0 and 4.

c. No. The reasoning here is the same as for part **b**. Lincoln's number is divisible by 3, so the only remainders possible when his number is divided by 9 are 0, 3, and 6.

d. No. The number is divisible by both 2 and 5 so it is necessarily divisible by 10.

e. Although this question is just like the others this is a much harder problem than any in parts **b–d**. We note first that 11 divided into 420 leaves a remainder of 2. It stands to reason, then, that 11 divided into 2×420 has a remainder of $2 \times 2 = 4$, and 11 divided into 3×420 has a remainder of $3 \times 2 = 6$, and so on. Then 11 divided into 6×420 has a remainder of $6 \times 2 = 12$, except that a remainder can't be more than a divisor, so we subtract 11 and get a remainder of 1, which is what we're looking for. So one number that is divisible by 2, 3, 4, 5, 6, and

7 but that leaves a remainder of 1 when divided by 11 is 6 × 420 = 2,520.

We are not through yet, for the problem asks for the *least* such number, and we have not proved that 2,520 satisfies this requirement. To do this is relatively simple, however. We reason as follows: The required number has to be a multiple of 420 because otherwise there would be a remainder when it is divided by one or more of 2, 3, 4, 5, 6, or 7. It was shown in the paragraph immediately above that the least multiple of 420 leaving a remainder of 1 when divided by 11 is 6 × 420 = 2,520; so 2,520 is the least number Lincoln can be thinking of.

Ask the students what the second least such number is, and see if they think they should be able to multiply 2,520 by one of the factors discussed (2, 3, 4, 5, 6, 7) or by 11 to get the answer. [I think the answer is 17 × 420 = 7,140 but haven't taken time to prove it yet. (I used 17 because there are 11 remainders possible—i.e., 0, 1, 2, . . . , 10—and 17 is 11 more than 6, which was the multiplier used above.)]

Page 179

This is a hard problem. I don't know whether or not this can be done in three weighings. Perhaps your students would like to look for such a solution.

326. When you remove balls from the pans, keep track of where they were. Also, when the scale is out of balance, notice the positions of the pans so that you can associate these positions with the balls the pans held.

First two weighings:

Place a ball in each pan and notice the scale position. Remove those two balls and repeat the procedure with two other balls. Remove the second pair of balls, too.

There are two odd balls. In the two weighings done so far, the two odd balls were either

   (1) weighed separately, or

   (2) weighed together, or

   (3) not weighed at all.

Suppose the scales were unbalanced both times. Then (1) is true, and the two unweighed

balls are normal balls. Either the pan positions were the same both times, or the positions were reversed from each other. If the positions were reversed, exchange the two balls in one of the pairs weighed so that if you were to repeat the first two weighings, the pan positions would be alike.

Third weighing for case (1):

Choose one of the pans and put into it the two balls that would be placed there if the two weighings were to be repeated. Put aside the other two balls that were already weighed. Put the two unweighed (known to be normal) balls into the other pan. If the scale is balanced, the odd balls are the ones put aside. Otherwise, you know which balls are normal for this weighing, and the odd balls are the other two. In either case, we are through.

Suppose the scale was balanced for both of the first two weighings. Then (2) is true or (3) is true and the scale would also be balanced if the remaining two balls were weighed.

Third weighing for cases (2) and (3):

Make a pair of the two balls that were weighed first. Make another pair of the two balls that were weighed second. Choose one of the pans and put into it one of these pairs of balls. Put aside the other pair just made. Put the two unweighed (known to be both normal or both odd) balls into the other pan. (Notice that the two balls in any one pair are equal in weight.) If the scale is balanced, the odd balls are the ones put aside, and we are through. But if the scale is unbalanced, then the pair of balls put aside are normal, and the odd balls could be either the pair that were previously unweighed or the other pair now on the scale.

Fourth weighing for cases (2) and (3):

One pan of the scale now holds two odd balls, and the other pan holds two normal balls. Replace one of these pairs with the pair that had been put aside. If the scale balances, the odd balls are the pair that was just now removed. If the scale is unbalanced, the odd balls are the pair that was left on the scale from the third weighing.

GLOSSARY

Words explained in the text are not listed here. To find the meaning of such a word, look in the Index for the page numbers where the word appears.

The definitions given here are as used in this book. See a dictionary for other definitions.

common factor—a factor that both of two numbers (or all of more than two numbers) have. [Examples: 2 is a common factor of 6, 10, and 18. 3 is not a common factor of 6, 10, and 18.]

contrapositive (of a statement "if P, then Q")—the result of exchanging and negating "P" and "Q." [Example: Given the statement, "If an animal is a tiger, then it has stripes," its contrapositive is, "If an animal doesn't have stripes, then it isn't a tiger."]

converse (of a statement "if P, then Q")—the result of exchanging "P" and "Q." [Example: Given the statement, "If an animal is a tiger, then it has stripes, its converse is, "If an animal has stripes, then it's a tiger."]

digit (DIJ uht)—one part, or component, of a written number. [Example: 6, 3, and 7 are digits of 637.]

distinct (dis TING(K)T)—all different from each other. [Examples: 2, 3, and 4 are distinct. The numbers in the set {4,5,4} are not distinct.]

factor of a number—a divisor (of the number) that leaves no remainder. [Examples: 3 is a factor of 12. 8 is not a factor of 12.]

integer (INT ih jer)—0 or a whole number or its negative. [Examples: -3, 0, and 138 are integers. These are not integers: -3.2, $138\frac{1}{2}$.]

power of a number—the value obtained by using only the number as a factor. [Examples: $5 \times 5 = 25$ is the second power of 5. $6 \times 6 \times 6 = 216$ is the third power of 6.]

prime number—a number other than 1 that has no factors except itself and 1. [Examples: 2, 3, and 11 are prime numbers. 1, 4, and 6 are not prime numbers.]

term—component or separate part. [Examples: Given the fraction $\frac{2}{3}$, its terms are 2 and 3; 2 is its first term, and 3 is its second term. Given a list of items, say

horse, bad-tempered old camel, baby elephant,

the list contains three terms, which are separated from each other by commas. The terms of a proportion are arranged like this:

$$\frac{\text{first term}}{\text{second term}} = \frac{\text{third term}}{\text{fourth term}}$$]

INDEX

© 1991, 1997 Critical Thinking Books & Software • www.criticalthinking.com • 800-458-4849